THE ANXIOUS HIPSTER

AND OTHER BARFLIES I'VE KNOWN

Grandma—
Thank you for being
such a big part of
my life!

Brian Amy

THE ANXIOUS HIPSTER
AND OTHER BARFLIES I'VE KNOWN

Brian Clarey

Cold Type
PRESS

The Anxious Hipster and Other Barflies I've Known

Copyright © 2011 by Brian Clarey

Published by Cold Type Press
Greensboro, North Carolina

Visit our website at www.lorraineahearn.com

Printed in the United States of America

McNaughton & Gunn, Inc.
Saline, Michigan

First Printing: November 2010

Edited by Elma Sabo

Book design by Elaine Shields

ISBN 978-0-578-07265-4

For Jill,
who knew all along

Contents

PART 6 – THE BACK NINE

EPILOGUE: THE GROWING SEASON

INTRODUCTION
THE ALL-NIGHT GRAD SCHOOL

Where I grew up, a few stops on the Long Island Railroad from Manhattan, newspapers were as much a part of the commuter culture as Budweiser tallboys in small brown bags.

I grew up reading guys like Jimmy Breslin and Jim Dwyer, hardscrabble city columnists who could turn a blacktop basketball game or a subway ride into a piece of poetry. I understood pretty early on that the reporters with their pictures over their bylines were a cut above. I wanted to be one of them.

But I was just another kid, finding my way through those crowded villages, bunched up like cigarettes in a pack, each one with its own pizza place, deli, train station, liquor store.

Long Island has a singular beauty, briny, windswept, turbulent. But in my mind, New York is always cold, tough, fast as the Atlantic smashing into that right angle created by Long Island and the North Jersey Coast. Like a bagel boiled in hard Brooklyn water, the people are thick-skinned.

To get anywhere as a writer, I needed something different. I needed out of the long shadow cast by the city. So I hit the road, to a place where the water is gentler and moves more slowly. At age 18, I headed to New Orleans. Enrolling at Loyola University was my cover story — but really I was after something else ... life ... action ... creative indulgence ... promiscuous women. And New Orleans was the place to find them.

Something else happened to me in New Orleans. I call it "grad school." I started tending bar.

I worked in little college joints first, pouring quarter drafts for trust-fund kids. But I got pretty good at it after a time, worked my way up the ladder, started laying cash into my pockets, and by graduation I had pretty much settled on a career behind the bar.

That's where I started to really talk to people — all kinds of people, from Crescent City aristocrats to beat cops to sob-story day drinkers with hairy forearms and crippling regrets. It's where I developed a work ethic based on honest physical labor and genuine demand, where I learned to read all the angles in a room and spot a hustle before it went down. It's where I found out how to give a guy the soft bounce with a smile on my face, where I discovered that everyone — even the homeless hangers-on and the crazy old dude talking to the ice machine — has a story to tell, and that sometimes a guy can pull a knife on you out of nowhere.

My time in the bars was an education in human nature. It's when I learned almost everything I know. And then things changed.

We realized the baby was coming just a couple of days before the Bartenders Ball, and the news of my impending fatherhood brought on the need for another big shift. I came out from behind the bar and once again discovered a whole new world.

In 2000, well before the floodwaters hit, we fled New Orleans with our two-week-old son for Greensboro, N.C., and the promise of a quiet, normal life — I still thought there was such a thing.

Things move forward. They take root and grow. Sometimes they bear fruit.

Now I'm a newspaperman, a bona fide columnist, documenting the city and its people, chronicling everyday dramas, trying to glean insights from the lessons life serves up.

I wrote the selections in this book between 2005-10, marking a time when I got serious about my career, watched my babies turn into full-blown kids and started cutting my own lawn. The pieces read much as they did when they originally ran in *YES! Weekly*, intended to preserve the urgency of deadline writing.

It's the kind of writing I like to do best. And doing it is much like tending bar.

So pull up a bar stool. Have a drink. I've got a great story to tell you.

Brian Clarey
Greensboro, North Carolina

December 2010

PART 1

THE STUFF OF
BARROOM MYTHOLOGY

The Anxious Hipster

He comes up to me at the bar.

"Hey man."

I turn to him and take him in, all earnest face and persimmon hair, clipped tonight into a Mohawk and sculpted painstakingly into Stegosaurian plates.

It's my friend the Anxious Hipster.

Our primary connection is the acquaintance of a wild waif named Casey, who paints a red streak through this town every few months and then splits for New Orleans until she comes back and does it again.

I know her from back in the day, though it's been awhile since I've had the pleasure of seeing her.

I haven't seen the Anxious Hipster in a few seasons either, so we spend a minute catching up.

Doing great, he gushes with characteristic gusto. Loves the job, loves the scene. Though he's quite drunk, the Anxious Hipster is more calm and focused than usual. He's been kind of lying low lately, busy at work and all … and remember that funny story you did? The one about the nine best places to swim in Greensboro and the one worst? Remember that?

I surely do, I say.

I'll never forget the day last June when Erik Beerbower, Greensboro's eminent mouthpiece for the arts, called the *YES! Weekly* offices in a restrained rage, tempered with humor. He was venting about vandals, skate kids or graffiti writers most likely, but definitely some species of disrespectful punk, who had one mild summer night on downtown Greensboro's main thoroughfare scaled the iron gate that shields Beerbower's River, the smallest body of water in town, from the action on the street.

The "river," a water sculpture Beerbower created, runs down an alley through a series of descending concrete ducts that swivels with the weight of the water. It ends in a pool just below ground level. The common wisdom at the time was that a skateboarder, unaware of details of the fountain's construction, hiked to the top and let fly, cruising until the third segment gave under his weight. It was unknown if the metal praying mantis sculptures — an integral aspect to the piece, in my opinion — were tossed in the collecting pool before or after this face-plant for the ages.

There would be justice, Beerbower assured us, whether as a result of a flier campaign offering a $250 reward or, perhaps, a reckoning meted out by the laws of physics.

"That's an 18-foot fall. The first thing I did was look under it to see if there was still somebody down there."

The tale has become something of an urban legend among the city's night people, retold by club hoppers on the sidewalks, discussed over tiny coffee shop tables and in dusty art studios.

A week later we named Beerbower's River the worst place in town to go swimming in our Ten Best feature.

"That was pretty funny," the Anxious Hipster says to me.

It was, I agree, pretty funny.

"In fact," I say, "I was just standing by that fountain today and I told that story."

The Anxious Hipster is quiet for a moment.

"You know that was me, don't you?" he says.

I tilt my head like a dog.

"That was you?"

"Yeah."

"I heard the guy broke both his legs."

"I shattered my heel," he says. "I fractured the other one. I still have a limp."

I have a rare moment of speechlessness. Then I say the first thing that comes to mind.

"What the dickens were you thinking?" Or something like that.

"I don't know," he says. "I just wanted to go up there."

It wasn't a skateboard thing or a graffiti thing at all.

After the fall it took four or five guys to get him over the gate, the Anxious Hipster says, including a couple of "homeless guys."

"My friends passed me over [the gate] to them and we gave them a couple of bucks."

And then he went home, only to wake with both his ankles swollen like overripe eggplants. He got a ride to Moses Cone — "the same [hospital] where I was born," he says — and began the road of recuperation, which included time in a wheelchair and, of course, legal accountability.

"There's still criminal stuff going on," he says, and he gives a slight wince.

But it's funny the way things play out. The Anxious Hipster's infamous fall put him out of action for months. He had been waiting tables, but after he could get around again he switched to kitchen detail to ease the strain on his busted-up feet. And he found he kind of liked it back there.

Today, just over a year later, he's the managing chef at the restaurant and eagerly studying the nuances of the culinary arts.

It was, he says, "one of the best things that's ever happened to me."

But it wasn't without its drawbacks. There are the niggling legal details, the occasional shooting pains that come from the bottoms of his feet ... and Beerbower will not return his calls.

But the Anxious Hipster's tumble down Beerbower's River actually tossed him into friendly currents. And it's made him the stuff of barroom mythology.

"I was standing in front of it the other day," the Hipster says, "and some guy came up and told me the story."

JUNE 20, 2006

Barflies I've Known

I've always had an affinity for bar culture, possibly because my family has its fair share of alcoholics, but I believe it's more than that. There's just something about a barroom ... a place of sanctuary and release ... where everyone's your friend, at least for a few hours, and the cares of the wider world dissolve like a sugar cube subjected to a slow stream of absinthe.

I like a bar even — or especially — when it's quiet: the hum of the beer coolers, the clink of ice in a glass, the gurgle of a liquor bottle poured at just the right angle. I like it when it's noisy, the perfect song on the juke and the bartenders slinging double time, and in the afternoon, when the workaday folks loosen neckties and watch the clock. I like it when the booze has saturated the crowd to that perfect juncture when everybody's had exactly enough and things start to get interesting.

A good bar can put you under its spell, a hazy reverie where conversation flourishes and the hours pass in quick-cut rapidity and the only thing that can break it is bright lights or a fight.

And I like the people who choose to spend their time in bars, the skirt chasers like Uncle Richie's nephew, whose favorite pickup line was, "Hey, we should go do it," and the red-faced old-timers like Oscar, the World War II pilot who got shot down on D-Day and then was requisitioned to lead a charge up Omaha Beach. That was his story, anyway.

I knew a lot of them in my time as a bartender in New Orleans, these lost and lonely, joyous and beautiful souls who chose to spend much of their time in the company of others, in a public house, sub-verting the rules by which the rest of us live.

I liked Crazy Jake, who used to talk to the ice machine, and Old Rick, who came down to New Orleans from Baltimore for Memorial Day weekend in 1957 and never left. I remember Big Bill, the proba-tion officer good for at least a bottle of Jack Daniels a day, taken in large pours over a light scoop of ice. There was South African Sean, a former Army helicopter mechanic living in the States on cash jobs; Good Guy Joe, who once lost his pants as he stood at the bar rail; the Finish Man, who likely still prowls lower Dectaur Street; Tyrone T, who announced before every trip to the bathroom that he was "gon-na go pay my water bill;" that one high-end prostitute who would drink a tall rum and Diet Coke, make her guy pay with a twenty, and leave me the rest.

How can I forget Manhattan John, Navy Dave, Cable Guy Paul, and Mikey in the Morning? And how do I even begin to explain Painless Paul?

There was nobody like Roger the Dodger, a Vietnam War veter-an who had beaten heroin addiction but still found himself itinerant on the streets of New Orleans.

I let Roger hang around the bar, gave him odd jobs to do, and sometimes tried to talk him out of his anger, which he generally car-ried around like a favorite pet. I once even got him a job, but Roger's homelessness was of the stripe that did not mesh well with the day-to-day responsibilities of consistent employment.

As far as homelessness goes, Roger had it pretty good.

He was among the most senior of New Orleans' street folk; at night he bedded down in the Piazza d'Italia, one of the nicest plazas in the Warehouse District. He was also conversant in the area's fine restaurants because he used to eat from their Dumpsters.

I once wrote a piece about panhandling in the French Quarter, using Roger as my guide. During my eight hours of panhandling, Roger showed me where I could use the bathroom without getting hassled, the best corners for flying my sign, and the stores that would accept coins as payment for booze, which was handy because about three hours into the experiment I started drinking.

When I left New Orleans, Roger helped me load the truck and stood on the street waving goodbye until we were out of sight.

He died a few months later, in the apartment of a mutual friend. My friend came home to find Roger's body on the couch, finally at rest.

There have been scores of barflies in my life over the years.

And it's not insignificant that a goodly portion of them have taken their last drinks — some of them by choice after years of the drinking life proved fruitless, others because they got 86'ed that one last time.

But it's good to know that some of them are still at it, drowning out the white noise of the world even as they solve all of its problems over drinks at the bar.

JUNE 2, 2010

COTTON

Cotton is not a hard woman to find, if you know where to look.

Park your car in the gravel lot, walk down a crumbling slip of asphalt that passes over the tracks, and follow a thin trail tramped down into the knee-high grass. As you approach the tree line, start calling her name. She'll hear you, but she may not answer.

Bring some tobacco — she prefers hand-rolled cigarettes — and a bottle of Mountain Dew, a big one. Maybe some Advil or something. She needs more than this, of course, but she'll appreciate the creature comforts. And this woman has done without the things she really needs for so long that an ounce or two of tobacco and a couple of cut-rate painkillers seem like manna from heaven.

She'll thank God for His blessed tobacco and expertly roll a smoke with her knotted but capable fingers.

"The tobacco has kept me from killing a couple a people," she says, "including myself."

She is not joking.

Then maybe she'll crunch one of those generic analgesics to ease the aches in her gnarled back, wash them down with a swig of the Dew. She'll pull down the smoke, carefully tapping the cinders into a glass apothecary lid she uses for an ashtray, pinch out the butt, and drop it into an old can that once held cherry pie filling.

She'll set the can on an upturned white cardboard box that is in pretty good shape; it serves as her nightstand, dinner table, craft bench. Perhaps, come winter, it will become fast-burning fuel in her quest to keep out the bitter cold that even here in the upper South blows through fast and hard.

Cotton doesn't have much; she lost her food stamps two months ago, she says, and she has trouble getting medication for what she calls "my ADD."

She has the clothes on her back: a Goodwill sweater in two cheery shades of green and the pair of Levi's she says she's been wearing since the advent of spring. She has her home, a domicile made of blue plastic tarp she got from a church and a few sheets and blankets salvaged from a Dumpster downtown, all elaborately tied together among the thin trees in this little thicket beside the railroad tracks. She has a few jugs of water lined up neatly by the entrance to her hut and a collection of empty Mountain Dew bottles, some fastened to a neighboring tree in a decorative fashion and others hanging from low branches, panels cut into their sides so they turn in the wind. She's got a knapsack full of keepsakes: a few extra pieces of clothing, a stack of business cards, a knife in a plastic baggie that may have been used in a stabbing a couple of weeks ago out here by the tracks, a green plastic watch running ten minutes slow. She has some smokes … for now. And she has a dog-eared copy of *A Separate Peace* by John Knowles. "Reading is my drug of choice," she'll tell you.

And she has the wheelchair, a narrow ironsides with thin wheels and a sloping seat parked next to her tent.

If she likes you, she'll let you sit in it while she tells you about her life: her childhood in Chicago, working construction in Texas, training horses out in California. She'll tell of running a couple of small businesses; working stints in bars, restaurants, and strip clubs; a couple years of college in Illinois; her two marriages, both doomed; four years in a Texas jail. She won't talk about the one child she birthed. "My life might be a fishbowl, but I wouldn't wish it on anyone else," she says. But she's candid about the last 16 years, all of it spent on the street, nine of it in the wheelchair.

"Sixteen years," she says. "People think I'm joking. It ain't no joke. People come out here and say, 'Glad to see you're doing all right.' Do I look like I'm doing all right?"

Residents call this place the Freeman Mill Campground, a privately owned piece of wilderness along the tracks of the Norfolk Southern line. It's in downtown Greensboro, a couple of hundred yards from city hall, our revitalized downtown, all those glass and steel monuments to order and prosperity.

There are maybe a dozen folks living hard out here by the tracks, Cotton herself won't disclose exactly how many — "I don't like to talk about my neighbors," she says — and they are but a fraction of the thousand or so homeless living within the city limits, though "homeless" doesn't quite describe the situation in which the residents of this campground find themselves.

Most of the men live on the far side of the path, over a Chain-Link fence a few feet into the woods. They've pitched tents in the clearings under the trees and built residences from found lumber and salvaged construction surplus. One, made from castoff roofing materials, looks like it could withstand gale-force winds. Clothes hang from tree boughs, drying in the fresh air. Jugs of water — for cooking, for washing, yes, for drinking — sit in the shade. At the base of one tree, many, many Budweiser King cans make a small, haphazard pyramid.

Cotton's place is across the way, tucked in among a few other sites. One tent over here exists in a small alcove created by the greenery, with a front yard of neatly raked gravel and an inviting sofa under the leaves. The woman who lives here lost her home to a fire a few months ago and was unable to collect on the insurance. Cotton's friend Don lives a ways around the bend in an orange and yellow tent he got from Walmart.

They find themselves out here for myriad reasons: mental illness, addiction, bad luck, bad timing, bad circumstances, bad attitudes. Some are unemployable, others just socially insecure. And some are like Cotton, who has been out on the streets so long she barely remembers what it's like not to be.

"Sixteen years is a long time, and there's no end in sight," she says. "I been laying out here dropping dead. I don't want a whole hell of a lot, but I need a little bit of something."

Don is a veteran, a former Navy fireman who saw action when helicopters crashed or torpedoes activated unexpectedly. He made castings for Chris Craft boats in Michigan and worked for a time in Alaska.

Now he collects cans and turns them in for cash. He hefts a 15-pound bag of them, crushed down for the weight.

"I can get maybe three dollars for it," he says. "It turns out to about a penny a can."

He spends many of his days volunteering at local homeless facilities, cooking soup, fixing things, offering counsel. Don likes to keep busy.

There's firewood neatly stacked between two thin trees at his site, a rebuilt bicycle leaning against another trunk, clothes drying in the trees like low-hanging fruit.

"Life was probably harder up in Alaska," he says. "You go out hiking, the land is unforgivable. You go out searching for someone, it could be whiteout, twenty below."

He's wearing a thin T-shirt and a pair of police-issue, navy-blue cargo pants. Shadows play across his gaunt face while a freight train rumbles along the Norfolk-Southern line. He says trains come by so frequently he's gotten used to them.

Don moved to Greensboro from Detroit because of the economy. "I researched it," he says. "I do an awful lot of woodworking, furniture and all that. I figured I'd have a better chance of employment."

Four hours after he arrived in town, after setting up lodging at the Greensboro Inn downtown, he was robbed of pretty much everything he owned.

"They took my ID and all that," he says.

With no ID and no fixed address, steady work is hard to come by. In three days Don turns 49. He's been out here about a year.

"So far, so good," he says.

Now he picks burrs off his pants and flicks them to the ground in front of Cotton's place.

"Don't throw those in the yard," she admonishes. He bashfully picks them up.

They're friends. Don brings her food when he can. Cotton says she hasn't left the campground but three times since April, and since her food stamps ran out she's been eating whatever she can get her hands on, including, she admits, some of the food people leave out for the dogs who run through these woods. Don helped her tie off the tarps for her shelter. He makes sure she has some staples. And he's handy to have around when things get tough.

Just a few weeks ago, Cotton says, a kid named Romero "got cut to pieces." She believes she found the knife used in the stabbing, has it in her pack in a baggie.

"I talked to the cops about it," she says. "They were supposed to come get it. I'd like to get rid of it."

Cotton has been attacked out here several times, the last resulting in kicked-in teeth and bite marks on her torso.

"The predator factor is awful," she says. "I been out here 16 years; most people wouldn't survive it. I'm here fighting grown men off with shovels."

This week Don made her a candle, a cylinder of purple wax in a Natural Light beer can; come winter it will bring the temperature up inside her tent a good 10 or 15 degrees. Now she throws a packet of tobacco to him, tells him it's his. He tries to give it back.

"Shut the hell up, Don," she says. "I wouldn't have jack shit if you weren't running all over town."

"You don't have jack shit now," he says.

But he takes the tobacco, slips it into the cargo pocket of his pants.

Cotton slept well last night. She rolls on the mattress in her tent about 11 A.M., runs a comb through her hair, and brushes her teeth.

"We're not totally heathens out here," she says. "We're just the same as everybody else; it's just where we live."

She pulls a couple of slices of wheat bread from a crinkly shopping bag, tears them up, and throws them out in her yard for the birds, which settle to the ground almost immediately for breakfast. The birds have names: Spartacus, Joseph, Fearsome. Sometimes, she says, a mouse comes and eats her castoffs. And there's a baby possum that often curls up in her tent with her while she's sleeping. She calls him Larry Gouda, "'cause he looks like a little cheese waddling around."

The animals keep her sane, she says.

Her morning meal is a couple of aspirin, some Mountain Dew, and some smokes. They seem to do the trick.

"This is the nicest place I've lived in for a long time," she says. "I guess I'll be out here until I drop dead or somebody helps me. If I had $500, I could get me some two-by-fours and I could make a place that's nice as could be, five feet wide, eight feet long, chop some windows in the thing … that would be like the Hilton for me."

The cold weather is coming; she can feel it in the air. When the time comes she'll winterize her home with extra tarps and blankets, lay in some more firewood and candles.

"A kerosene lamp," she says, "that'd be the ticket. But who can afford it?"

And soon the Downtown Greenway will cut through this patch of woods and grass, displacing all who scrabble for survival here.

For now, she rolls another smoke, flicks it, and drags deeply while another train rumbles past.

"It really sunk in about the hobo camp the first time the train came by," she says. "I was like, 'What the heck am I doing out here?'

"That railroad bridge looks pretty appealing to me some days. You know what I mean? You can't imagine how discouraging it is to see the light at the end of the tunnel, but it keeps blinking out."

October 7, 2009

Battleground Boutique
Beckons Botox Babes

I have been to frat parties. I have been to balcony parties. I have attended costume parties, wear-a-stupid-hat parties, ecstasy parties, Super Bowl parties, tailgate parties, lingerie parties, spur-of-the-moment deck parties, vomit-on-your-suit parties, dance parties, and release parties. I've even been to a baby shower where a fistfight broke out. But I'd never been to a Botox party.

Until yesterday.

The scene was Diona's Boutique, an upscale (but not too upscale) clothier recently relocated to the stretch of Battleground Avenue that also includes Plato's Closet (basically a Goodwill store for teenagers and others more hip than me) and the busiest Biscuitville in town. It is also the natural habitat for a particular stripe of Greensboro's hot moms.

"We moved here about two months ago," says Diona, a lithe blonde who is the best advertisement for the clothes she sells. She's trim and curvy, but possesses a shrewd businesswoman's sense of supply and demand and also a keen eye for a trend.

The Botox party was her idea.

"I had heard about them," she says, "and we inquired with the doctor to see if he could do one."

They've been holding these things for about a year now out of Diona's. Every two or three months — approximately the same suggested interval as Botox upkeep treatments — they have one.

The doctor is running a bit late this afternoon, so the ladies sip wine, nibble cubed cheese and chocolate kisses, and talk on their cell phones. ("That house is absolutely to die for," a well-dressed woman says to a far-flung friend. "To die for.") But mostly, the women shop. Manicured, Pilate'd, hair-dressed, they browse the displays of short dresses and snappy tanks in the multicolored hues and bright palettes of spring. The metallic slide and click of hangers on stainless steel racks evoke in me a memory of the marathon shopping trips across Long Island my own bargain-hunting mother would drag me on when I was too young to have my complaints acknowledged. I instinctively look for a chair as Tammy Styers, a store assistant, directs customers to the dressing rooms, all named after American centers of fashion.

"You want to go to Vegas today?" she asks a customer, arms laden with the latest couture. "Right this way."

The MD, David C. Best of Best Impressions Plastic Surgery in Greensboro, arrives in a modest burgundy SUV and hustles a Styrofoam cooler of Botox to the back room of Diona's. He's an unassuming man with big tortoiseshell glasses and a few tufts of facial hair. He looks a bit like Frank Oz, though he doesn't have the funny voice, and the next time I see him he's got a needle in his hand and he's saying things Kermit the Frog never would.

"You're going to feel a little sting," he says to the first patient of the day, a dignified blonde in an animal print skirt. "We'll do the crow's feet area first." And back here, amid the mannequin torsos and form-shaped hangers, he leans over and injects the needle through about five pages' worth of skin to the thin muscle that governs the squint instinct. The Botox, which Dr. Best says is derived from the bacterium that causes the form of food poisoning known as botulism, attaches itself to the nerve endings that govern muscle twitch, harnessing the paralytic side effect of botulinum toxin A to deaden the impulse. The muscle goes slack and the surface wrinkles disappear until three months or so later, when connection between muscle and nerve tries to reestablish itself and the Botox must be administered again.

"This is mechanically simple," the doctor says. "It's not a facelift, not a tummy tuck. It's basically a chemical blockade tool."

A Greensboro matron and mother of five grown children slides into the chair in the back room of Diona's. Her first time, she was brought in by her best friend, and she's visibly nervous.

"It looks like it hurts," the woman says, wide-eyed.

"Well," the doctor replies, "there is a needle involved." And he runs down the history and science of the procedure, effectively (though not totally) cooling her jets.

The doctor turns his back and fills the syringe with Botox. The woman and her friend hold hands.

"Everyone's gonna say, 'You look so rested,'" the friend says. "[They'll say] 'What have you done?'"

The doctor bends over his patient and gains purchase on the thin skin with his fingertips. He makes the shallow injection.

She winces. Shuts her eyes. Slides her foot on the floor. Says, "Okay okay okay okay okay." When it's over her eyes are watering, but she's still in one piece.

The next patient is a bit more cavalier, a suntanned, bob-haired blonde who seems as comfortable with the procedure as she is with a trip to the hairdresser.

"It's summer," she says to the doctor. "God, can you do anything about my thighs?"

She pays the medical assistant and leans back in the chair, shuts her eyes. The doctor fills the needle and bends over to administer the dose. She takes a long, slow breath.

"Make it go away, daddy," she says, and he slides the needle home.

MAY 10, 2005

Leroy Jenkins and His
Traveling Crusade of Healing

The Asian woman gets up from her seat and sidles to the aisle, leaving her two children with the assembled flock. Her daughter, maybe 10, watches her with wide eyes.

Mommy's done this before.

By the time the woman reaches the fissure in the wide rows of chairs on the floor of the Guilford Ballroom, she's near brimming with the Holy Spirit, or some such thing. She's in a plain white linen dress with a diaphanous purple sash tied across her chest. Her black hair is in a simple plait and her feet are bare, callused, and strong. The feet of a dancer.

She puts them to use when she hits the aisle, expressing herself and her love for the Lord in interpretive dance with eyes shut tight as a well-dressed organist lays down a funky spiritual on his Hammond B3.

Her young daughter, also in white — a Communion dress, it looks like, paired with a set of pearls stranded with a silver chain around her neck — follows to the back of the room and tries to talk her mother out of her reverie, though the kid likely knows that almost nothing can bring Mommy down from this holy high.

Mommy brushes her away and continues her frenzied dance.

People are starting to stare. And there are hundreds of them in here by now, clad in Sunday best and weekend wear, zoot suits, sweat pants, fancy hats, T-shirts, and at least one dashiki — a rainbow of pigmentation and ages and cultural pigeonholes, and a few genuine hotties.

They watch as a security guy in a red shirt corrals the Asian woman, secures her in a double chicken wing, and ushers her out the door.

He hustles her past the wheelchairs — more than a dozen of them, both motorized and manually operated, with small treaded wheels and big thin ones, low seats and high backs, a few tricked out with hooks and racks for feeding tubes, oxygen hoses, and intravenous drips.

The wheelchair bound are here, not unlike the Asian woman, to be filled with the Holy Spirit courtesy of the Rev. Leroy Jenkins, and more than a few of them hope to rise from their carriages this afternoon and leave the building under their own power for the first time in ... forever.

Jenkins is a man of God whose faith is made manifest by the power to heal, something he's been able to do, according to his website, since the summer of 1960, after his right arm was nearly severed in a household accident and the Rev. A.A. Allen performed a miracle of God at the Atlanta Fairgrounds, restoring the limb to full utility.

The site does not say that he's also an ex-con, with a slew of drug and booze arrests and a conviction, in 1979, on two counts of conspiracy to commit arson (one to the home of a South Carolina state trooper who gave his daughter a speeding ticket).

But he made parole back in '85, before his marriage to a septuagenarian lottery winner (annulled in 2001), and has more or less stayed out of legal trouble, save for the state of Ohio's mandate that he cease distribution of water from the well on his property, water which Jenkins says is capable of catalyzing miracles but which the Buckeye State claims is contaminated with harmful bacteria.

You can buy the stuff for $2 a bottle right here, from a guy at a side table. Forty bucks gets you 24.

It's moving. Many of the assembled flock have cases of the stuff, which is packed in white boxes with a monochromatic portrait of the holy man on the side.

Jenkins is about to make his entrance.

"He's a healer; he's a prophet," says the hype man. The flock erupts. "Go on, go on .... He's the real thing."

And he takes the stage, clad today not in one of those rhinestone Elvis suits he sometimes wears but a black tuxedo with peaked lapels and a wing-collar shirt. And he's singing a song about Jesus — how much we love Him, how much He loves us.

The security team has told the Asian woman, who now sits on a bench in the hall, that she can come back in if she promises not to dance. She's on the bench, eyes shut tight, her arms and legs still working to her internal rhythm.

No deal.

It's apparent by the arch of his eyebrows and the slant of his eyes that the reverend has had some cosmetic surgery. He affirms this with an opening salvo that invokes the early days of his ministry, the cost of travel, and, yes, a plug for his plastic surgeon.

"If you can look better longer," he tells the flock, "do it."

Praise God.

It's just one of many pieces of counterintuitive wisdom he drops this afternoon.

On the lottery:

"I don't know if it's a sin or not, but I'll tell you one thing," he says. "If I can put a dollar down and win ten million, I'm gonna do it. People say, 'That's the devil's money.' I say, 'I know, and he's had it long enough.'"

On evangelist preachers:

"Somebody's got to stop these hypocrites," he warns. "If those people don't go to hell for charging people [money] to go to church, then there is no hell."

On the nature of God:

"I don't like what I do," he says. "It makes me sorta mad that

God tricked me. He said, 'I'll heal you but you'll work for me forever.'"

On his own merchandise:

"I got some tapes and books back there," he tells them, "but they ain't gonna help you. They may comfort you. But all you need is this Bible right here. Take it out and read it."

There are more than one thousand people in here. Not a bad draw for a rainy playoff Sunday.

In the wheelchair section a young woman fills a feeding tube with milky stuff from a can and a bit of Jenkins' miracle water. The tube runs into what seems to be her husband, who is settled into a high-back wheelchair, one with a headrest. His left arm is trembling. His right one lays still.

"There are seventy-three men here today with prostate cancer," the reverend proclaims from his pulpit. "How do I know? Because God showed me some of them."

He leans down to address a couple in the front row.

"Ma'am?" he says. "You want your husband to stand up? He was talking about me before you came, wasn't he? He don't believe I can do it."

The husband stands, burly with white hair, blue shirt, and red suspenders. In the manner of a Vegas mentalist, the reverend establishes that they do not know each other. And then he tells the man he has prostate cancer. The man tearily nods.

Jenkins has the man drink a small vial of the miracle water and then he lays the touch on the man, a hand on either side of his head, makes him repeat an affirmation.

"I am healed. I will never die of cancer."

Jenkins goes on to restore a woman's hearing, anoint a young man to the ministry, remove a cancerous spot on someone's lung, and induce an elderly woman to stand from her wheelchair, dance a tiny jig, and walk across the room.

The young wife in the wheelchair section holds a hand-lettered sign: "I challenge you." She neglects her post only long enough to wipe something from her husband's chin.

Jenkins stops the music abruptly.

"There's gonna be five minutes of the Holy Ghost flowing through," he says. "You're gonna see people getting out of wheelchairs, throwing canes up in the air."

But first he lays down another touch, this one on the entire room.

"Imagine everyone that you were just given a thousand dollars," he says. "I want you to reach in your billfold, get your checkbook, and write a check for as close to a thousand dollars as possible. Maybe it's a penny. Maybe it's a dollar. The closest you can get to a thousand, whether it's a quarter, nickel, or dime. You gonna be blessed. And some of you very unexpected."

Congregants choke the aisles on their way to the collection baskets in the front of the room by the stage. And everyone who donates gets the privilege of standing up there, right near the man as he wraps up the afternoon.

"I ask that God opens the windows of heaven tonight and pours you a blessing," he says, and the crowd stands with arms raised, eyes shut, and faces tilted upward. Even the sound guy is doing it. And there are tears of rejoicing and voices high with passion. As the funky get-down builds to a crescendo he intones, "I love you and may God bless all of you and your families. Thank you so much."

A new moment. A new chord. The reverend sings the recessional, a tune made famous by both Frank Sinatra and Elvis Presley: "My Way" — except that traveling each and every highway is done, in this case, "God's way."

Somebody praise Jesus.

And then the flock make for the doors in a slow crawl, their movement impeded by all the wheelchairs and walkers.

JANUARY 9, 2007

Big Pitch

Phil Town paces like a panther on the squared platform at the center of the Greensboro Coliseum. His back is broad under the jacket of his fabulous dark suit; his thick shock of salt-and-pepper hair holds a soft wave; his jaw line makes a perfect square.

His shiny shoes cut a swath through a ground covering of confetti, ejaculated when former New York City Mayor Rudy Giuliani took the stage an hour or so earlier to kick off the Get Motivated Business Seminar, this all-day event that has got the Coliseum buzzing like an orchard hive in spring.

They've been flogging it on the airwaves for weeks with buzzwords and name drops: Business! Leadership! Motivation! Rudy Giuliani! Colin Powell! The guy who landed his plane in the Hudson River! You could get a passel of tickets — enough for your whole office — for less than 20 bucks. And the place is packed. Traffic on Lee Street played hell with the morning commute; the parking lots are full at $10 a pop. Inside, seating areas on the floor and the mezzanine and the upper level teem with ambitious humanity: middle-aged men in golf shirts and pleated pants, cadres of note-taking women, entrepreneurial types, and many who wear the forlorn look of the recently unemployed.

They're here to get fired up ... or, at least, get a glimpse of a man who ran for president. But I'm not here to see Giuliani. What did the guy do, anyway? Gentrify Alphabet City and run the hookers off Times Square?

And you can forget Colin Powell too. I don't need a lesson in leadership from a man who gave false testimony to the United Nations at the behest of his Peter Principle president. Lord knows what the guy would say for a paycheck.

Besides, anyone can report on whatever canned remarks these two jokers might give. The real action is in the undercard — the speakers who underwrite the entire venture for a chance to get some face time with the crowd of hooples, perhaps 15,000 strong, after they've been primed to action by the marquee names and motivational speakers on the bill. I'm here to see the Big Pitch. And right now Phil Town is spinning a work of art.

"You've got to think about what you want," he's saying. "I mean, do you want a CLK350?" Silence.

"That's a car, people," he laughs. "Well … does anybody out there want a new pickup truck?"

This is answered with roars from the assembled. Town holds his hands out wide.

"My people!" he exclaims. "I got a Ford F-350 dually pickup," he says. "King Ranch."

They're listening. He quotes from the gospel according to Warren Buffett regarding "margin of safety," and intones well-timed aphorisms: "Eighty-five percent of the money in the stock market is managed," "The big guys can't do it because they're too big," "This is not rocket science."

The PowerPoint slides click off on the big foursquare screens above the stage and positioned at each end zone — stock charts and performance charts and market estimates and indices. And that's not all: There are photos of Town on horseback, strapped into a snowboard atop a snowy peak, astride his Harley-Davidson in Sturgis.

"I like to ride horses and snowboard," Town says, and it's hard for him not to be smug. "This is how I pay for it."

You think he needs to be here? Phil Town is rich, bitch. Even if he didn't stack so much paper from the market, he'd still be rolling on the cash. His *New York Times* bestseller, *Rule #1: The Simple Strat-*

egy for Successful Investing, throws off. Rule No. 1, he reminds you, is, "Don't lose money." Phil Town could buy your whole neighborhood. He could kick your ass, too. Phil Town was a Green Beret and a river guide. And he could probably bang your wife — that is, if he hasn't already.

He lays the pitch: an investment system that uses an automated software package and clear indicators, which look like green arrows on the stock chart, delineating the perfect moments to buy and sell. It's a system based on market timing and incremental gains to generate cash flow, and he says he maintains his own fortune by using it for about 20 minutes a day, beating the big investment funds every time.

And then he makes his proposition: a two-day workshop held by *Wealth Magazine* valued at $1,995, and it just so happens there are nine of them running right here in the Triad between May 30 and June 9; online tutorials that will show you how to use your home computer to build your fortune, normally $995; and a three-month subscription to *Wealth Magazine's* online investor toolbox, which would normally run you $149. That's a $3,139 value, folks, but as a special deal for participants in this seminar, he's going to drop the price of the whole package down to $299.

Still not interested?

Well how about this: If you are willing to sign up today, right now, for this incredible batch of products and services, Phil Town is going to give it to you for just $99. Out in the concession ring, long tables hold graduated stacks of clipboards, each holding a pen and a contract for the Wealth Magazine Investor Education program with the listed price of $299 crossed out and a handwritten "Only $99" underneath.

And they stream from the arena, bunch around the tables with hands outstretched, snapping up clipboards like each one is the last pancake on the platter, copying down Visa numbers and filling out checks.

The rest mill around the concession ring, buying $8 box lunches, scanning the crowd for familiar faces, lost in the rapture of imagined fortunes, yearning for a bigger and better deal.

The crowd is a pickpocket's dream. But picking pockets is a loser's game. In the end, it's a lot easier when they give it to you freely.

JUNE 3, 2009

DELUSION AND FOOT SWEAT: MAKING FUN OF MODELS AT THE MALL

There's a lull in the action just after lunchtime at High Point's Oak Hollow Mall, according to Joe Sigman, director of promotions for WCWG, the Triad's CW Television Network affiliate.

"We were doing like forty or fifty an hour for the first two hours," he says before dashing off to consult with the line of preening young women that is once again starting to grow along one of the mall's pillared halls.

They're here, each and every high-heeled one of them, to become the Next Big Thing, or at least to take a shot at it, as Sigman and his crew screen hopeful contestants for the hit show "America's Next Top Model."

They're here to be judged solely on their physical appearances. And that's exactly what I intend to do.

It's a real scene, man. These chicks have come from as far away as Queens, N.Y., with a healthy contingent from Georgia and plenty of local talent to fill out the ranks. Joe is expecting more than three hundred to pass through the chrome-plated corral, show their profiles on the camera, and do their best catwalk in the hopes of getting berated by television crazy lady Tyra Banks and her band of vacuous nasties.

There are rules, to be sure, clearly outlined on the WCWG website, though many of these hopefuls have neglected to read them. You need a driver's license and a Social Security card. You need three photos: a close-up, a full-length clothed, and another in a swimsuit. You must be at least 5 feet 7 inches tall. And, of course, you must be beautiful in a model kind of way.

Still, Sigman says, of the first 135 participants, "forty of them didn't have what they needed. One girl drove all the way from Georgia, but she was like five-four. She turned around and drove back home."

And some of these broads have got to be kidding me: the beer guts ... the eye bags ... the blurry tattoos. It smells like delusion in here, delusion and foot sweat, and I'm asking myself if any of these trash-glam wannabes have ever even seen the show.

But wait a minute ... there's one, a tall, willowy number with teeth like Chiclets and the kind of slim, athletic build that routinely gets high school gym teachers fired. But hold the phone. Upon closer inspection I notice that her facial skin has some blemishes and barely discernible patches that mar her otherwise uniform tan.

Next!

Models are freaks of nature, you know. The American concept of beauty is based on bilateral symmetry and proportion in both the face and the body with emphasis on the slopes between armpit and thigh, and the simple fact is that people are not built like that. Most people, frankly speaking, are trolls. Ever been to the state fair? Yeah, like that.

And the pickings here are not much better, even though the crowd is stocked with people shooting for supermodel status. Seriously: the home perms and bad dye jobs, the square asses and FUPAs and bulging hips, those cankles, that back fat, those big noses ... wait, scratch that. I like the girls with big noses.

And, hey ho, what about that one? The one in the simple cropped top and real short skirt worn low on her glabrous abdomen, with the concave stomach and those protruding hip bones? Hip bones are the new cleavage, you know. She's all right ... but ... wait a minute ... there's a bit of a double chin issue there, and now that I'm looking closely I can see that she's got something of a jowl problem. And what's up with those eyebrows? Such a shame.

This one's too pink; that one's too pale. This one is slouching. She's too dark. Her friend is not black enough. That one looks like she got smacked in the face with a frying pan, and this other one forgot to wax her treasure trail.

There's a gallery of perverts watching from the upper floor, leaning over the railing and straining their vision, and more than a few teenage girls are watching from up there, too, with stars swimming around their wide-eyed faces.

Oh, there are a few hotties in here, to be sure: classy hot, Nubian hot, stripper hot, innocent hot, big-booty hot, MILF hot, ghetto hot, hipster hot.

And look at that one, the leggy yellow blonde ... but her dress is suspiciously puffy, like she's hiding something. There's another in a baby-doll dress and leggings to her well-toned calves. She's got nice legs, nice shoulders. But she's got a bit of the crazy eye. And here's a contender with a square-cut page-boy 'do, risky in her $200 jeans and expensive jewelry. But then I catch her from another angle and see that she's got one of those low-slung drop-seat asses that might work well bent over a coffee table but isn't up to snuff for "ANTM."

Next!

March 28, 2007

THE BREAK-IN

It was late. Pre-dawn darkness late. Scary late.

I was in bed laying down the kind of snores that compels my wife to wear earplugs at night. She was enjoying her own fitful slumber. Our sons were tangled in a mess of sheets and blankets on a mattress at the foot of our bed, a treat reserved for weekends and the rare weeknight when there's something really good on Cartoon Network. They were dressed in their superhero costumes, Spider-Man and Mr. Incredible. Across the hall our daughter sawed some wood of her own — she snores just like her daddy — in the tiny bed that she graduated to on her second birthday.

Things, it seemed, were as they should be. But most assuredly they were not.

Because in the precious early-morning dusk, the slice of the day that once belonged to me and my rambunctious crowd, those hours, we used to tell ourselves, when absolutely anything was possible and when the weirdest shit always seemed to happen, there were things ... people ... conspiring against us. They were right outside our bedroom window. And they were trying to get in.

My wife heard something through her earplugs that, God bless 'em, failed to live up to their advertised properties. She sat up in bed.

"What are you doing?" she asked in the darkness. "Go back to bed."

Later she tells me she saw a head by the window. She thought was our son.

She woke me up.

"I think someone's trying to get in the house."

And though I generally sleep like I've got a head injury, that did the trick.

How many men like me fear hearing those words more than anything else? How many of us sometimes lie awake at night replaying such a scenario over and over? How many of us have nightmares about an unseen and malevolent force creeping among the ones we love and the home we've made? How many, when we even think about it, feel our hearts fill with rage and limb-numbing fear?

And when it all goes down, what the hell are we gonna do about it?

I woke quickly, tried to stay quiet as I fumbled for my glasses and slid them on. I crept to the edge of the bed and saw two of my babies still sleeping on their pallet on the floor. I looked and saw the blinds swaying lightly in the window frame. The sash was wide open.

I leaned to the floor and found my pants right where I'd dropped them before I crawled in bed. My phone was still in the pocket. I pulled it out, dialed the magic number, and handed it to my wife.

I slipped from under the covers and got the only weapon within reach, a fraternity paddle I keep on the top shelf of my closet.

Yes, I was in a fraternity. Now is not the time.

My wife had the 911 operator on the line while I moved towards the open window, rearing back with the sturdy wood paddle, picturing the dent I could make in a man's head with it, wondering if I had the balls to do it.

I saw him. I saw the motherfucker, the tips of his fingers as they separated the blinds and allowed a slash of light to play across his right eye.

I reared back again.

"Get the fuck out of here!" I said.

My wife told me later how scared I sounded. But I guess it did the job.

There's more to the story, of course. My room to room search, flicking on lights and attacking shadows. Checking on my daughter and nearly weeping with relief to see her undisturbed. My window screen lying mangled in the grass in my backyard like a bird that had been shot down in flight.

The Greensboro Police Department, it must be said, responded in a few short minutes, though those minutes were the longest of my life. To the credit of the force, the crime was solved before the sun came up.

Thanks, guys. If we ever get a good night's sleep again, it will be in no small part to you.

The perpetrators were teenagers, though not unfamiliar with the penal system, and their pre-dawn confession will put them at the mercy of the justice system.

My wife and I are talking about getting a gun. Or a dog. Maybe both. We're certainly going to increase security measures in our house and our yard. Today.

We're scared. The "what-ifs" are piling up like garbage in my house. Underneath them is the certainty that one more illusion we held about the world is gone.

MARCH 14, 2007

Way of the Gun

From out in the parking lot the gunshots barely even sound like explosions. They're more like muffled slams, like a sledgehammer hitting a tree. There is no sharpness to the report, no crack or boom.

They keep butterscotch candies and Jolly Ranchers in a bowl by the front door at Calibers Indoor Range in Greensboro and pepper spray under the glass. Paper targets lie in bins by the wall, and the bullets are in shelves behind the counter.

They don't sell guns at Calibers. You can't even rent one unless you're one of the club's 4,000 members, a new policy necessitated by a nationwide shortage in ammunition, which Calibers does sell. Many theories exist as to the cause of this ammunition shortage. Some say the world's many armed conflicts are taxing the supply, or that U.S. gun owners are hoarding ammunition because they fear domestic terrorism, martial law, or, even scarier, gun control laws. Carl Abbe, who bought Calibers five years ago, isn't buying any of it.

"They said people were hoarding, and then they said the manufacturers couldn't get the materials, the metals, and powder." He shrugs his shoulders.

He says it's true, though, that the election of President Barack Obama marked an uptick in the gun business. Before the election, he says, they would sweep up six buckets of brass bullet casings each day from the floor. Just after it, they were regularly sweeping up nine. Enrollment in Calibers' concealed-carry permit classes is up as well, Abbe says; about eighty percent of those enrolling are first-time gun owners.

This jibes with national and local statistics regarding concealed weapon permits. North Carolina is on pace to double the number of such permits issued in 2008. Guilford County had issued 1,151 concealed permits through May, compared with 1,965 in all of 2008. Forsyth County issued 1,305 permits in 2008 and has already licensed 1,088 of its residents to carry concealed firearms this year.

"I don't think it's political," Abbe says. "I think it's mostly for their own security. They think for whatever reason the police can't protect them adequately, and they decided to protect themselves."

Greensboro, he says, is "having a hard time controlling their crime."

Don't I know it. My own neighborhood has been the locus of much crime. I have heard gunfire at night, seen a shooting in the street, been carjacked in my front yard, chased burglars from my bedroom window.

There are many times when I see arming myself as a reasonable proposition. The way of the gun is the way of the world — or so it seems.

At the shooting range, I watch an eight-minute video outlining the rules of the house: no quick-draw, no outside ammo, no kneeling, no swearing, and a mess of gun safety policies.

Abbe asks me the question he asks everybody who comes to him wanting to buy a gun for self-defense: "Would you be able to shoot without hesitation a 14-year-old with a gun pointed at you? How about a 16- or 17-year old? That's what could potentially happen," he continues. "If not, you need to find some other means of protecting yourself."

Attendant Manny Matos sets me up with a .38-caliber Smith & Wesson and a full box of loads; he brings me through the doors to the shooting gallery and positions me in a stall. He tapes my target — a silhouetted human torso with a big bull's eye on the chest — and runs it ten yards deep. I load a single shot in the chamber, line up the sights, and dry-click the thing until it explodes with a jolt.

It's the first time I've fired a gun. It feels like a firecracker going off in your hand, except the firecracker is huge, and your hands are made of steel, and you can aim at a target and blow a hole neatly through it. I reload and pop off six shots, the last two clustering in the bull's eye.

Manny pulls his personal piece, a .357-caliber Magnum, more blunt and muscular than the .38. He loads a single bullet, hands it over, directs me to shoot. I pull the trigger.

The report is big enough to shake my bones, and the kick stresses my triceps and latissimus dorsi. It blows back, and I can feel the concussive force in my sinus cavity. Shooting a .357-caliber Magnum is like all the best parts of getting punched in the face. It's awesome.

I look to Manny through my protective eyewear. He's nodding slowly and smiling at me as he holsters his gun.

JUNE 10, 2009

RAIN ON THE CASTLE

Rain falls on the castle near the foot of Summit Avenue. It rolls off the roof and trickles from the eaves, runs through the gutters and drainpipes. Rain slinks down the castle's hard granite surface, rivulets racing to the mossy ground, where they seep into the soil.

The castle has stood guard on this corner since William Vaught built it in 1906, a bulwark against the expanding center city back when this was "Silk Stocking Road," when this stretch of urban gentility was what passed for a suburb in Greensboro.

The windows have gone dark in the castle's apartments. Everybody moved out within the last year, and now the house is on the market.

Maybe somebody will want to put a law office in there, or a web-based business. Maybe — just maybe — someone will want to live there again.

The house is quiet, but it tells a story. The black smudge on the alcove facing Charter Place suggests fire; the empty rooms bespeak silence; the way people look at it when they walk or drive by implies fear.

Something terrible happened on the ground floor apartment just a year ago. A violent beating. A sexual assault.

A murder.

And it happened in the Saturday morning stillness of the Aycock Historical District, with neighbors walking to the farmers market. William "Ransom" Hobbs was murdered in this castle some time around 8 a.m.; his hostess, Deborah Ann Moy, was brutalized and beaten. Both were set afire in a blaze that scorched the floor and blackened the ceiling in the center of the room.

Hobbs was likely dead before the flames took him. Deb Moy was not so lucky. It's been a year since the fire in the castle. Hobbs has been mourned and remembered, and his name still comes up just about every weekend at the Blind Tiger when the band plays a certain song or the night hits just the right level of absurdity that Hobbs would have appreciated. And Moy exists inside a triangle of fear, excruciating pain, and incalculable mental anguish as those who love her hope desperately for a reckoning.

It's been a year since the vicious attacks took one life and broke another, and yet the case remains much where it has been since the beginning.

Greensboro Police Detective Tim Parrish lives with this case, its details committed to memory, its victims part of his everyday vocabulary.

He says he's made progress in the collection of evidence. He's been able to reorder a list of primary suspects and has gained enough perspective to be able to look at the case in a different light. But the handcuffs stay put.

"It's moving slowly," he admits. "I'm sorry, that's just the way it is. … We just continue to look at this stuff. It's not what I want — I don't want to move slow. You move at a pace that's comfortable and try to do things right."

An arrest in this case is one thing, a conviction quite another. It takes evidence to get a conviction, and most of the physical evidence has already passed through the fire.

"It's the most frustrating case I've ever worked," Parrish adds. Still, the barrooms are abuzz with possible suspects, pet theories, barely remembered fragments of that Friday night when Moy decided to host an after-hours party for a select few friends and acquaintances.

"I thought it was her ex-boyfriend." "What about that dude she was dancing with?" "It's totally messed up." Even a year later, at the bars and parking lots, in the wait-stations of Greensboro's restaurants, the talk turns to the fire at the castle, the murder of Hobbs, the fate of Moy. And the unspoken fear can still send a jolt through the community: Whoever did this could still be walking around the city. It might be someone at the bar or someone I work with. And it could have happened to me.

Still, the beers get filled and the tables get bussed. The people who remember Hobbs celebrate in his name and grieve in a way of which he surely would have approved, while those around Moy tighten their circle and look for spiritual reassurance. The grisly episodes come and go in Detective Parrish's caseload. And rain continues to fall on the castle, to give a chill to the granite façade, and to scatter sounds in its empty rooms. It falls like whispers. It falls like tears.

SEPTEMBER 23, 2009

LAST-MINUTE REPRIEVE

It's just another sunny January morning, or so it seems through the sepia-tinted picture window of my cheap motel room — muted winter sunlight warming the kudzu and a circulatory hum of traffic emanating from the nearby city loop.

Just another morning in the Old North State, except I'm in this perfectly serviceable room with its thin queen-sized mattress and that print on the wall, a watercolor depicting a quiet pastoral scene in the foothills, a bare and gnarly tree dominating the foreground. It's quiet and a little bit lonely — I sorely miss my wife and kids — and I've got a little pot of coffee brewing on the bathroom sink while I tap at the keyboard at this pre-fab desk with empty, shallow drawers.

And I'm washed in a feeling akin to sweet relief.

Because it's just another Friday for me, close enough to the weekend that I can almost smell the bacon frying and looming deadlines causing mild anxiety. But it could have been something much, much worse.

I drove out on I-40 yesterday afternoon, a passage I know well from my days as a travel writer. I don't hit the road so much these days, but this was an assignment I could not refuse.

Through a short chain of events I had obtained one of the toughest tickets in town: a seat in a room I imagine to be not much bigger than my modest temporary lodgings where I would bear witness to the last moments of Marcus Reymond Robinson. Death. By lethal injection.

Robinson was not a real good guy in the bad old days. He and trouble were well acquainted when, with his equally loathsome pal, Roderick Williams, he shanghaied Erik Tornblom on July 21, 1991, in Fayetteville, forced him to drive to a field, and then blew away his face with a shotgun.

Robinson and Williams each fingered the other for the actual shooting, but it was Williams who got the deal — a life sentence — while Robinson got a date with the needle.

And that's today.

Or it was. A judge put a stop to the madness.

It's kind of a long story. The state requires a doctor to be present at all executions, but a few weeks ago the N.C. Medical Board stopped playing ball. It stated that doctors should not participate in the lethal injection process, effectively dropping a turd in the punchbowl of state-sanctioned death. Now a judge has put executions in North Carolina on hold until ... I don't know.

But the upshot is that what's just another January morning in the Triangle is the first day of the rest of Marcus Reymond Robinson's life.

For now.

I do not support capital punishment for many reasons, among them the fact that it's possible to hang the wrong man. Daryl Hunt was but one of hundreds, if not thousands, who have had a murder conviction overturned.

But I also find the notion of the state committing murder in my name to be distasteful. I don't think any human has the right to hold sway over the life or death of another living human, no matter what.

Though Erik Tornblom's family might disagree.

But when the assignment landed in my lap, I could not remit the opportunity to see the draconian measure go down.

It was a spooky notion and one that didn't sit well with the inner recesses of my mind. I kept thinking about it, visualizing the sequence of events and trying to predict my reaction, both my immediate one and the toll it would take on my psyche over the years. Even my wife was having dreams about it.

All these years after the crime has been committed, Robinson is still, by most accounts, not such a good dude. He is known as an "active rioter" at North Carolina's Central Prison, just around the curve of I-440 from my modest quarters. His prison sheet includes incidences of assault, gang involvement, various drug offenses, fighting, lock tampering, and (yuck) throwing liquids.

Yesterday, when he sat in his cell in the deathwatch area of Central Prison, maybe thinking about his chances at the pearly gates or attempting to atone for his sins or maybe just thinking about the menu for his final meal, he was given another chance at life, though it's likely only a temporary stay of execution.

It's difficult to say whether he will make the most of it or not — his profile suggests he won't, though I've never met the man and can't presume how this brush with eternity will affect him.

But I know I'm breathing easier this morning, despite the deep infestation of tobacco smoke in my generic little room, because I, too, got a last-minute reprieve.

JANUARY 30, 2007

Cotton Grows Indoors

I brought Mountain Dew, a big bottle of it, and a pouch of cheap tobacco. She had taken a swig and was rolling a smoke before I sat down in the chair by the window.

Cotton's got a place of her own now, what might generously be described as a studio apartment at the former luxury hotel now known as Heritage Homes. She's got a bed — a mattress, actually — pushed into the corner on the floor and a couch that's a bit ratty but still perfectly fine for sitting on. By the window there's a small desk loaded down with paperbacks. Her windowsill is filled with plants in soda bottles, and in her sink she's making a little wine in two glass jugs.

"It's just grape juice, sugar, and yeast," she says. "It's actually pretty good."

She's even got a new wheelchair — a *newer* wheelchair, anyway, with a seat that doesn't slope forward, wheels that still grip, and a chassis that still shines like chrome.

"They were throwing them out at the nursing home," she explains.

There's a full bathroom where she can shower regularly, a small kitchenette suitable for all kinds of things other than bootlegging, and eastern exposure that allows the morning light to stream through her single window. And there's a lock on the door, just in case someone thinks about invading her jealously guarded privacy.

"Mostly the neighbors are pretty nice," she says. "They mind their own business."

Oh, things aren't perfect. Not by a long shot. She's here by the grace of her disabilities, both mental and physical, which qualify her for free rent, but she's got no source of income, no transportation save for the chair she's been confined to for the last 10 years, no phone, no computer, nothing to do all day but read paperbacks, repurpose cigarette butts, and wait for the wine to come around.

It's better than the Freeman Mill homeless camp where she lived when we met, but it's no weekend in Vegas either. Take this week. She got hustled trying to exchange her food stamps for cash — 50 cents on the dollar — so she could buy things not covered by government assistance: tobacco, for one, which she says has saved her own life more than once. Toiletries like soap, toothpaste, and toilet paper — she's currently using as bath tissue pages of a book titled *Making the Most of Your Money.* Cleaning supplies. Kitchen items like plates, cutlery, aluminum foil. Birdseed — she likes to feed the birds. Aspirin. Band-Aids. A cheeseburger. And books. Books, she says, are her only escape.

She's working her way through Arthur Hailey's *Airport,* the story of a troubled airport manager trying to land planes in a snowstorm. She has not been on an airplane in many, many moons, but she knows something about snow. She survived the past 16 winters on the streets, the last couple in a tent by the train tracks on the Norfolk-Southern line. She has known — still knows — frustration and despair.

But things definitely look better from the second floor of Heritage Homes.

Yes, in an economy that seems to be pushing most people downward, Cotton is one of the few who is upwardly mobile — a new set of castoff clothes here, a suite of scavenged furniture there. A lot of things have fallen into place since we last met in the parking lot of Greensboro Urban Ministry where they still let people smoke.

Of course, to say things have fallen into place belies the struggle she's endured, like a prehistoric marine animal lurching from the ocean, crawling inch by inch on land and gasping to take her first breath.

She's got some breathing room now. Things are better. But still she's got empty pockets to contend with, a disability that keeps her confined to her wheelchair, virtually no hope of employment or anything resembling complete self-sufficiency. And then there's that copy of *Making the Most of Your Money* on the sink in her bathroom, disappearing one page at a time.

"What do you think?" she says. "You think someone would sponsor me for like, fifty, a hundred bucks a month? Do people do that?"

"I don't know," I say. I truly don't — even the logistics of such an arrangement are beyond my ken. I tell her so. She shrugs, pushes herself off her couch, and hoists herself into the wheelchair.

She wants more books, and she knows just where to get them: the free pile in the corner of Edward McKay's, where she'll load up a dozen or more musty paperbacks: thrillers, romances, biographies, mysteries. I'll take her there myself. It's the least I can do. Up here, on the second floor of Heritage House, where the houseplants grow in sawed-off Mountain Dew bottles and the wine is cooking in the kitchen sink, every little bit helps.

SEPTEMBER 1, 2010

PART 2

JUMBO SHRIMP

A Steady-Rollin' Man Comes Full Circle at the Flat

What's a guy like him doing in a place like this? It's a Thursday night, for one, and "Steady Rollin'" Bob Margolin is a Saturday night kind of guy. He didn't spend his green years seated at the right hand of Muddy Waters, sucking it up and throwing it down, to be the opening act on a freakin' Thursday. In a basement bar in downtown Greensboro, no less — the Flat Iron, subterranean headquarters of the city's hipster, musician, and general inebriate quotient.

Everybody knows this guy, right? One of the last true practitioners of old Chicago blues? Guitarist for Muddy Waters' band in the 1970s? Contemporary of Johnny Winter, Taj Mahal, insert-your-favorite-influential-blues-artist-here? C'mon! The guy was in *The Last Waltz!* And if you know of him, you probably also know that Margolin lives in Greensboro, is very much a part of the local blues community, and has been known to take gigs with some of the up-and-comers in small music halls around the Triad.

So maybe it's not so strange seeing Margolin on the Flat's abbreviated stage leaning into his well-seasoned ax while the crowd grows deep enough to make the walls bulge. On a Thursday.

A voice from the bar shouts: "Who were your influences?"

"I wanted to play the guitar because of Chuck Berry's music," Margolin answers.

"And you, the nice young lady at the bar."

"How did you get the nickname 'Steady Rollin'" she wants to know.

It's a long story involving Muddy Waters, a college radio DJ, and a cut by the Robert Johnson Trio made way back in the day called "Steady Rollin' Man." After telling the tale, Margolin launches into his own version of the tune that gave him his name. "I'm a hard-workin' man," he sings, "have been for many years."

Amen, brother.

Margolin is no stranger to rooms like this, with beer rings on the bar tops and smoke gathering in the corners and well-used whiskey bottles that pour all night long. After his stint with Muddy came to an end in 1980, the Steady Rollin' Man spent the decade working the mid-Atlantic bar circuit in booze-soaked rooms where the blues is more than just a chord progression.

"It was about the music," he'll say, when people ask. "There never was a whole lot of money in it."

Tonight on stage he remembers Greensboro's Nightshade Café. "Oh man. The place would get full-up, the ceiling was just a few inches overhead, the Chinese restaurant was upstairs. I really miss those kinds of places and those kinds of days," he says. "Thank you for bringing it up." And then, just like on an episode of VH1's "Storytellers," he launches into "The Thrill is Gone," which you've got to know is a Roy Hawkins tune and not just something pretty that B.B. King makes with Lucille.

Margolin prefers the Hawkins version, which allows him to play chords. He plays a tight lead and then messes with the meter, something he picked up from the Mud Man, creating this pocket … and then he's in it, bending the neck and stretching the strings in a solo that starts like gently falling snowflakes and ends like a blizzard.

The notes hold power, enthralling some and inspiring others. All the guitar players in the room try to pinch these licks.

And then Margolin comes full circle, laying into "Johnny B. Goode," the number that made Chuck Berry — and, by proxy, Bob Margolin — a star. On bass is Stan Atwell, a Greensboro attorney who is one of 12 musicians who have signed up to sit in with the legend.

Atwell's exhilarated. "I felt like I kept up," he says later, "but really it was about the chance to play with Bob Margolin."

After the show there's whiskey and cigarettes and beers as the band members rotate on the stage, each trying to pay tribute to Greensboro's most famous bluesman who tonight has come full circle in his own hometown. To them it's a moment for the ages.

Margolin keeps a cool head. "I don't think I'm very famous," he says afterwards. "To be well known in the blues world is like being a jumbo shrimp."

JULY 23, 2008

A Late-Night Date
with the Hedgehog

Here's the deal: If Ron Jeremy comes within 50 miles of my house, I'm gonna go see him.

I have my reasons.

Ron Jeremy is the most prolific male porn star in history, with almost two thousand roles to his credit and another couple hundred which he directed. It's enough work to earn him the title of Top Porn Star of All Time by *Adult Video News* magazine, and his body of work — and his actual body — speak for themselves.

The guy's famous, more than just porn-star famous, though if his adult film career, which was launched when a girlfriend convinced him to pose for *Playgirl* magazine, was the beginning and end of his legacy, he would still be considered kind of a big deal.

And he's not just a big star — he's a ... big ... star, endowed well enough to be able, in his lithe and limber prime, to perform the act of autofellatio.

True, I was a kid when his first pornographic film, *Tigresses and Other Man-Eaters,* was released in 1979 and, honestly, though I've sat through as much porn as the next guy, I don't believe I've ever seen a Ron Jeremy film in its entirety.

No matter. I still want to meet the guy and, if possible, have my picture taken with him. You know ... for Christmas cards or something. So I make short the trek east to shake hands with the Hedgehog.

The scene is Club Kryptonite in Burlington, N.C., one of those dimly lit dance halls where the women shimmy on tabletops and the action doesn't get hot until midnight or so. There are elevated dance platforms with stripper poles, a VIP lounge that looks a bit like Fred Flintstone's house, and mirrors everywhere.

I get there early, a couple of hours before the Hedgehog, and watch footage of Saturday nights gone by on the big flat-screen. The images are almost exclusively of women ... more specifically, a certain stripe of woman who looks good in tiny clothes, devotes her weekends to binging on Red Bull and vodka, and considers it socially acceptable to perform the pelvic grind — to music! — with other similarly clad women and the occasional male who is able enough to wrestle his way to the bar top.

The door opens and the room begins to fill as the Asian bartenders preen and the doormen, who look like they've been constructed from bowling balls, adjust the short sleeves of their skin-tight shirts. Short skirts, diaphanous eveningwear, and booty jeans make themselves heard, and a crew of women have come clad only in underwear and thigh-high, lace-up boots. Watching them are a bevy of guys who ritually apply cologne and ChapStick.

And they swing into action, these minions of the dance floor. Grind! Bump! Do the robot! Look at my crotch!

Ron Jeremy is gonna love this place.

Steven Harvalias, who created Club Kryptonite with his father, Manolis, says the Hedgehog's appearance almost never went down.

"We've been trying to get him forever now and we couldn't," he says. "It was honestly just out of our price range."

The tipping point came when the Hedgehog made a visit to a whiskey stronghold south of Myrtle Beach called Suck Bang Blow and father and son realized the extent of the man's popularity.

Manolis says Jeremy will earn $10,000 for his appearance, way more than he made for his first hundred or so pornos.

"I think he's a huge draw," Steven says. "Look: People are already flocking in."

They are.

"There are a lot of women in the house," he continues. "He's a huge women draw and a lot of guys who envy him."

And here he is.

The video screens show Jeremy exiting an SUV in the parking lot in real time — mustache, greasy locks, forearm hair, and all. He's mobbed from the moment he walks through the door and makes his way to the DJ booth.

"Hey everybody!" he intones, and delves into a stand-up schtick that includes self-deprecating semitic humor, oral-sex jokes, and a piece of prop comedy.

I try to get a moment of his time, but he waves me off.

And then he wades into the crowd, posing for pictures, autographing breasts, nibbling ears, administering wet kisses and loose gropes. Women love him. Nattily-dressed brothers love him. I'm smiling, too.

I'm at the bar a few minutes later when I feel a tap on my shoulder. It's Jeremy, pulling a suitcase full of swag behind him. He hands me a Polaroid of him cuddling a baby tiger and then pulls out glossy photos; T-shirts that show him in his studly prime; rolling papers that bear his likeness; and copies of his book, *Ron Jeremy: The Hardest (Working) Man in Showbiz,* which, he shows me, shared space on the *New York Times* Bestseller List with a book by Bill O'Reilly. He sets them all up on the end of the bar, and now he's got a minute to spend with this intrepid reporter.

"Why do women love me? He echoes the question. "Because I'm an average guy getting gorgeous girls," he says plainly.

Average? I think not. Put aside his prodigious member for a moment, and it's important to note that Ron Jeremy was once Ron Hyatt from Bayside, Queens, who held a master's degree in special education from Queens College. And forget for a minute all the porn he's done and try to remember that he's done television, music videos, and PETA ads. He even addressed the Oxford Union debating society in Great Britain.

And it's not irrelevant that, by his estimation, he's had some form of sex with between two thousand and three thousand women. And counting.

"I get more ass now," he says, "because I'm more famous now."

MAY 22, 2007

Seven Minutes of Funk
with Mr. George Clinton

Do I want to interview George Clinton? *Do I want to interview George Clinton?* You damn right I want to interview George Clinton, the godfather of funk, the Atomic Dog, the Supreme Commander of the Mothership. I want to talk to that guy as long as I can keep him on the phone.

I came relatively late to the P-Funk party — indeed, I didn't make my funk a P-Funk until 1988 or '89, when I fell into the funk canon by discovering the Neville Brothers, the Meters, Chocolate Milk, Sly Stone, and that really tight James Brown stuff all in a matter of weeks when I was a college freshman who was beginning to tire of classic rock and the Grateful Dead. This was just after the granddaddy of the groove was championed by the Red Hot Chili Peppers for "Freakey Styley" but before the gangsta rappers began sampling his stuff for their ghetto anthems. Clinton moved between the two worlds as if they were one — which in his mind they were.

"I learned a long time ago style wasn't all that there was," he told me by phone from a hotel room in Providence, R.I. "Wasn't anything hipper than nothing else. It was all a face."

I'm kind of just assuming that this quote backs up my assertion. Because there's something you need to know about Clinton: The dude is out there. Way out there. And his mind works on levels that my own has yet to achieve.

Plus, I have a hard time understanding what he's saying. And I don't mean that in a metaphysical sense. Guy talks like he's got a mouthful of marshmallows. Funky, funky marshmallows.

"Yeah, yeah, bawerzibop," he says to me. "Great show last night. Great. Got some brand new fans upanatee. We get a new crop every year."

OK, I can do this. Clinton was born in Kannapolis, N.C., and lived in Maryland, Virginia, and Washington, D.C., before settling down in Newark, N.J., to play music and open a barbershop. The music was of its time: Motown-influenced doo-wop. The group was named the Parliaments. After the cigarette. But it was the barbershop, the Silk Palace, that enabled him to make real inroads in the music business.

"We was processin' heads," he says, "zemmafugee. We makin' folks cool. Make a man lamanabe a pimp. And so did the preacher! Ha! … In Newark, most of the pimps and players and musicians came in to get their hair done. Jackie Wilson, the Temptations. Yammamono. The Playboys jaymee from New York, too. Zattaboogafee.

"Rammatta," he continued. "Oh yeah, you hear a lot of the bullshit in the barbershop. You know, lyin' and signifying and talkin' shit. Manassas. You got a lot of the music stuff, and a lot of subject matters camongeree. Everybody was always talkin' shit in the barbershop."

Clinton has always been something of a hustler, working the music business by "creating" different bands, with different names and sounds, to play on different labels — though most of the bands were comprised of the core members of Parliament, the spaced-out groove machine that came to embody Clinton's philosophy in life as well as music.

Clinton always has let fans record his performances, which always seem packed with jam-band kids.

"Yabame," he says. "It's more like a grassroots type of thing. They tape and basically trade those things. It don't hurt sales or nothing."

The convoluted path led to royalty and copyright issues at times in his career, but Clinton does pack houses even now, in his 67th year, as he tours in support of his new album, *George Clinton and*

Some Gangsters of Love. It's a slate of covers with guests that include RZA, Carlos Santana, his old friends the Chili Peppers, and Sly Stone himself.

"Zhagadda," he says. "I got some of the obscure songs, barax I don't want wadunda. We kicked the ones that was mostly in the 'hood or in the affanama. Oveggane of the songs you might never have heard unless you were black in the ghetto."

Gangsters includes "Gypsy Woman" by the Impressions, Marvin Gaye's "Ain't That Peculiar," and "Never, Never Gonna Give You Up" by Barry White.

"Yeah," he says, "this whole album is full of that. That old dada-mada. That big sound."

I want to know more about his band, his music, his life, and I'm starting, I believe, to speak the language of funk just a bit more fluently. But Clinton cuts the interview short.

"Homone," he says. "I got amajanee on the other line."

George Clinton clicks off.

July 15, 2008

HOOTERS INVADED
BY HUNGRY WRESTLERS

Balls Mahoney looks like he could run through a brick wall.

Check that. Up close, Balls Mahoney looks like he has run through a brick wall. But for now he's barreling with a graceful, big-man's gait through the large crowd that's assembled here at Hooters, making his sweaty way to the bathroom after he's taken down a rocks glass filled to the rim with what looks to be a margarita, no salt, no ice.

He's friendly and gregarious, Mahoney is, and he gets and gives backslaps and clinches when he's outside the perimeter of the area Hooters has cordoned off for him and his friends, the group of professional wrestlers that has just finished slamming the crap out of each other at the Greensboro Coliseum just down the road.

I bet you didn't know that professional wrestlers, after they strip off their spandex and shower off the detritus of a good night's grappling, like to head for the nearest Hooters and take down some beers and wings. I didn't. But I probably could have figured it out.

Kori Martes, who has been serving chicken wings in tight clothes for about eight months, was on duty the last time the wrestlers came in.

"I mean, everybody was here," she tells me. "It was like Wrestling 101."

Tonight they enter through the side door in trickles: Jimmy Wayne Yang with Little Guido Maritato, Tommy Dreamer and Matt Striker, CM Punk, Matt Hardy. They're wearing ball caps, ponytails, tattoos, and beards. There are sternocleidomastoid bulges in their T-shirts, and a bit of showtime intensity remains in their eyes.

On the tables, plates of shrimp, wings, clams, fries, fried pickles, burgers, and chicken sandwiches pile up in short towers. Pitchers of beer and tall, iced Cokes are drained with brio.

Kelly Kelly eats wings demurely, a zebra-striped hood obscuring her young and fresh face. She sits with a couple other World Wrestling Entertainment divas and with Hornswoggle, the league's littlest fighter. Mark Henry, the widest, most solidly built human I have ever seen, holds court on the outside patio. And then there's my friend Mahoney, who can tell me he's from New Jersey but little else. The various professional wrestling entities are fairly protective of their talent and forbid unapproved interviews.

Which is fine by me. I'm here to dig the scene, this frenetic and star-struck sequence unfolding in Hooters on this Tuesday night.

The fans jostle and crane to see their heroes from outside the perimeter of the zone, and occasionally one slips through for an autograph, a squeeze of a perfect bicep, a moment captured on a phone. The gladiators are gracious, rubbing elbows and sharing tales of the ring, signing autographs and Hooters menus, making faces for the kids.

But they gotta eat, so Tommy Dreamer, who is known as something of a heel, hustles the hooples out of the corral.

Dreamer, one of many ex-New Yorkers in professional wrestling, is perhaps best known for being the first person in wrestling history to kick out of Jimmy "Superfly" Snuka's Superfly Splash. Guy's been around forever, worked his way up through the business and is now something of a statesman in the sport.

Matt Striker, too, has risen to prominence in the league after resigning from his job as a New York City schoolteacher in 2005. A bit of controversy there. Striker took 11 sick days during one semester so he could wrestle in Japan, and the school district sought reimbursement for the time off.

The educator thing has stuck with him as part of his wrestling persona: He lends his face and skills to the WrestleMania Reading Challenge, which encourages reading among teenagers, and acts as spokesman, with CM Punk and the Miz, for Teen Read Week.

He's the only one wearing a suit — "Because I make more money," he says — and he's not afraid to throw around his heft, both intellectual and physical.

"From one educated guy to another," he tells me, "these guys see you writing things down ... they don't know what you're doing. If I were you I might not be here."

Striker's duress is interrupted by the arrival of the Edge, one of wrestling's prototypical golden faces. He's huge, of course ... chiseled and cut, with a Hollywood visage and kind, wide eyes framed by blond locks and a knitted toboggan.

He's major. In 2007 he beat the Undertaker (with a little help from Henry) to become the WWE World Heavyweight Champion, only to lose the title to the Undertaker at WrestleMania XXIV.

Now he makes his way past the fans, signing a few menus and posters, posing for photos with the waitresses and greeting his comrades in arms. Striker brings his dinner: a piece of plain broiled fish and a similarly prepared chicken breast. When the adoration hits a lull, he hunkers down and protein loads as Striker looks on.

APRIL 29, 2008

CHITA RIVERA AND BRIAN CLAREY, TOGETHER AT LAST

What the hell does a guy like me say to Chita Rivera?

Frankly, our names don't even belong in the same sentence, let alone the same room.

A quick review of our respective bodies of work:

She was trained as a ballerina at a young age and used that discipline to become one of the biggest stars on the Great White Way. My background is in booze and video games. The two have done me little good over the last 25 years.

Rivera performed in the original Broadway productions of *West Side Story* and *Bye Bye Birdie*. I was an inaugural member of the mug club at the Loyola University campus bar.

Rivera has been nominated for eight Tony Awards, winning two of them, and was presented a Kennedy Center Award by President George W. Bush. I was named "most improved goalie" at Adelphi University Soccer Camp in 1978 and "best sports writer" in a college journalism contest for a piece on a female personal trainer that was shamelessly loaded with sexual innuendo.

At 73, Rivera has the legs and ass of a 35-year-old. I am beginning to be concerned, at 36, about varicose veins.

Yet she still conceded to a phone interview, and even over the long-distance line I was intimidated.

"I'd like to ask you something you've never been asked before," I say to her.

"Good luck with that one," she says.

Rivera received rigorous training at George Balanchine's School of American Ballet in New York City. So I open with that.

"Ballet shaped my career," she says. "It's got everything to do with the foundation. Certainly that's what I tell all the kids: Without ballet training, longevity is not the same; the body is not the same. You can only build a house with a good foundation. If something goes wrong, technique takes over for you and saves the day."

But surely her success has something to do with the roles she's chosen. Right?

"I can't say I picked them," she says. "The door was open and I was smart enough to go through. When you're asked by Fred Ebb, Bob Fosse, Michael Kidd, all those great choreographers and directors, you're kind of foolish not to take it."

She likes writers, too.

"The writer makes a good character. Passion. An edge. A darkness. In the case of *Birdie,* a sense of humor. Naturalness. It's the writer; the writer makes the character interesting. All these kids on stage today think they can write their own script. I want to speak the writer's words — don't leave it up to me. I can ad-lib, but I want the writer. You gotta speak the writer's words in exactly the way he wrote them, and in rehearsal if they don't work that writer will change them to fit."

This unlikely senior citizen also advises up-and-coming female performers to eschew the term "diva."

"I hate it. I see that as kind of a ... it's nothing. They've given that word an attitude. It was originally given to a great, great, great opera singer. That comes with experience and talent and time. Now, whatshername ... I can't even think of these young kids' names ... the poor girl who was lip-syncing on TV and her sister."

"Ashlee Simpson?"

"Yes. Now Christina Aguilera is a brilliant singer. But she's brilliant. But the Simpson girls ... They probably give the Hilton girls the title of 'diva' these days. I just loathe it."

As far as advice for the whippersnappers, she is blunt.

"All I know is to work hard, to respect your work, respect the actors you're with and not to be alone. Don't think you're out there by yourself — listen to the director. It's a collaborative feel; collaboration is a very important thing. When you're young you just listen and do: That's how you learn. Don't think you're better than everybody else. They should have the freedom and the courage to show themselves, to give of themselves to the craft. That is the only way you find out who you are and the only way to find out what talent you've got — not by copying anybody, but by being yourself. Have a passion for your work — there's no easy way out. You gotta work hard."

Perhaps the only things Rivera and I have in common are the acceptance of hard work as an ingredient to success and a loathing for the Simpson sisters.

NOVEMBER 28, 2006

TNT: Good Times
at Green's Supper Club

The fallen star, Jimmie Walker, sits at his table on the upper deck at the live entertainment lounge in Green's Supper Club. He's still got his jacket on.

There's a fireplace painted on the wall and fake bricks brushed atop real ones. An overhead light fixture casts a yellow spot on him.

People are looking at him. Talking about him. Pointing. He is, after all, the man they've come to see — the onetime television star of "Good Times" whose catch phrase still resonates some 25 years after the cancellation of the show. He's used to people staring at him, even now in his late fifties with his head filled out like a soufflé and flecks of silver stubble in his recently shaved scalp.

He's scraping the last bit from his baked potato when a reporter approaches and asks for an interview. He looks up from his plate with an expression of tolerant annoyance and mumbles something dismissive. The reporter backs away.

Jimmie "JJ" Walker, star of stage, screen, and radio, doesn't like to be interviewed. It says as much on his website, dynomitejj.com, in the FAQs under the heading "Worst things about being on the road." Four of the five concern people who ask questions for a living. As for the print media, he writes, "They never print what you say … they have their own agenda … and don't do their homework."

What it doesn't say on his website, the substance of a rumor buzzing around the journalistic types, is that he's touchy about the catch phrase — he doesn't want to talk about it, won't use it in his act. And we'd heard that it would be highly unlikely for him to spit it out for a fan or interviewer.

"Jimmie's been in show business a long time," his manager told me. "There's some things he's kinda funny about."

Walker's career has spanned almost 40 years, since 1967 when he landed a gig opening for a militant poetry group called the Last Poets. He broke in when Bette Midler and others used their influence to get him on late-night TV. Things happened quickly from there: a "Laugh-In" appearance, a TV pilot, bigger and better club dates.

Then Walker made his mark in a new Norman Lear sitcom, a groundbreaking schematic depicting an African-American family living in the Chicago projects. He was at the first rehearsal just goofing off when he uttered the phrase he'd carry around for the rest of his life.

DY-no-MITE!

Things are not exactly explosive tonight at Green's Supper Club. Patrons from all over the county chew prime rib and oysters while sitting through the opening act. Walker takes the stage as the "Good Times" theme blares through the speakers.

"Keepin' your head above water, makin' your way when you can."

He takes the stage underneath a plastic banner that says "Reidsville Nissan" and spreads his arms wide.

"It's come to this, has it?"

He gets a pretty good laugh.

Walker's character in the old show, James Evans Jr., was an aspiring artist. "Van Gogh, and Rembrandt, don't be uptight, cause here comes KID DYNOMITE!" he once enthused.

Walker the man is something of an artist himself. He's been doing standup a long time, and tonight his timing, his transitions are impeccable. He's even got some fresh material, written about events that happened this very day, and you can still hear the rasp in his voice that once made him famous when he says things like "manual mammogram" and "the runaway bride."

He closes with some football jokes and gets off the stage with the crowd still laughing, making his way quickly to the back of the room. As he passes a table, a guy in glasses looks up at him and yells, "DY-no-MITE!"

Walker keeps moving.

In the back room by the piano Walker signs T-shirts with an old picture on the front and dated photos of himself holding actual sticks of dynamite. One of each is going for 20 bucks, and the wad of cash in Walker's hand grows by the minute.

"We loved you in that show," says one woman before she leaves with an autographed T-shirt.

Another woman, this one in a suede coat, runs up to the signing table.

"I just gotta hear you say one thing," she says.

Walker ignores her, talking instead about football to a guy in a wheelchair. She stands to the side, fiddling with her purse. She's not giving up easy.

He finally acknowledges her.

"What are you looking for, young lady?"

"I gotta hear you say it," she says.

Walker drops his voice to say something inaudible to the rest of us and the woman looks crestfallen. She argues.

"I can do whatever I want," he says, and his voice drops even lower.

She makes one more plea. Walker gets serious.

"That was a long, long time ago," he says.

The woman looks down at her feet. Then she leaves, quickly and quietly, out the door.

NOVEMBER 1, 2005

Part 3

Ports of Call

Goin' Back To New Orleans

"Wait 'til you see the lakefront," Atom says.

We're at the airport, the one renamed for Louis Armstrong back in the '90s, loading our stuff into Atom's trunk. From the tiny windows on the plane we saw the Federal Emergency Management Agency tarps on the roofs, casting them a joyous shade of blue that has become — along with purple, gold, and green — one of the official hues of the city. We saw the ruined roof of the Superdome, now two-toned like a black and white cookie, where desperate people took refuge in the days following the storm. And we saw the enormous expanse of Lake Pontchartrain bisected by the causeway that crosses it to the North Shore, calm and blue, with boats leaving frothy wakes on the surface and people clustered in groups on its shores.

But at 9:45 a.m. on Aug. 29, 2005, this body of water turned hostile, crashing through the wall atop the 17th Street Canal and turning the tawny Lakeview neighborhood to a toxic soup bowl.

This was not the only engineering failure on that day, but it was one of the worst. Water flowed through this breach and inundated huge chunks of the city faster than water rising in a bathtub, sending people to their attics with chainsaws and hatchets (and, I heard, pocketknives) to cut through the roofs. The unlucky ones succumbed to the rising waters. The lucky ones … well … there weren't too many lucky ones. Even the survivors had to deal, are still dealing, with loss of property and way of life.

But we're on more or less dry ground now with Atom and Nat'ly. They're my friends. It turns out I have lots of friends left down here.

It doesn't surprise me. Once you love life in New Orleans with all your heart and soul, nothing else will do.

And a quick word about attribution: We don't use last names in New Orleans, often because we don't know them even with people we've been around our whole lives. But first names work just fine down here, and in a pinch "Darlin'," "Sweetheart," or "Baby" will do.

On the ride from the airport we pass the 17th Street Canal, and we can see the neighborhoods that exist well below the waterline. When I lived here, cabbies would point this waterline out to gawking tourists on their way into town, this aquatic Sword of Damocles, this constant reminder that we were all just one serious rainstorm away from obliteration. It made the tourists nervous, but the locals used to laugh about it … one more absurdity of life in New Orleans.

Of course, no one's laughing now.

The road to Lakeview is clogged with poorly driven cars. The date palms have been stripped of fronds, and the once-lush magnolia trees retain just a fraction of their waxy green leaves. When we reach the neighborhood, the "Lakeview" sign, once a proud proclamation of a privileged area in one of the most poverty-stricken cities in the country, is surrounded by clumps of brown weed. Its letters are faded from both the scorching Louisiana sun and the floodwaters, which reached higher than 10 feet in some parts of this neighborhood.

But more visually striking is the damage to the homes, the price points of which would have once started in the mid-six-figure range. You can see the watermark, left like soup skin on the side of a pot, sometimes a few feet off the ground, sometimes a few feet over our heads. Some homes are crushed like accordions, some crumbled like cardboard. The sturdy brick ones have been hollowed out by gusts of water; some of the wooden ones, built in the New Orleans style on top of concrete blocks, have been lifted from their moorings and pushed to the interior of the block. Some are reduced to piles of rubble. There are FEMA trailers in many front yards — this is a neighborhood on a long, slow road to recovery

Atom's been working days out here gutting houses when he's not tending bar, but the frequency with which he sees the damage does not blunt its effect on his psyche.

"It still makes me cry when I come out here," he says. "When the waterline's up to the ceiling … it's all these people and it's all their belongings and they're mush. You can't salvage these people's things. There was this old lady and she was looking for her deceased husband's Purple Heart from World War II. I found it for her, but just the medal part. The rest was mush."

We pass by a neutral ground near the canal, once a grassy divider between well-traveled roads now reduced to a dump site and parking lot for heavy machinery. Atom pulls the car near the breach that allowed so much of the lake into this neighborhood. The home right near it, once a gay pink stucco and brick domicile, bore the brunt of the flow. Now an entire corner of it is gone, and the roof is twisted and buckled like a sick joke.

Across the street the U.S. Army Corps of Engineers has placed a temporary steel Band-aid over the failed section of levee wall. There are no workmen here, no machinery, and the area by the girders is not roped off. We can walk right up and touch it if we like.

The next hurricane season starts on June 1, 19 days from now. And counting.

Friday afternoon at the Old Absinthe House on the corner of Bourbon and Bienville streets and it's hard to tell that the city received a near-fatal blow less than a year ago. Under vintage NFL helmets that hang from the ceiling, the bar is three, four, five deep. The bartenders sling Sazeracs, Ramos Gin Fizzes, and the house drink, the Absinthe House Frappe, to the tourists. The local professional crowd, a mainstay in this barroom for generations, stick to vodka drinks and beers. Some of them have been drinking since the hours-long liquid lunch at Galatoire's, a downtown tradition that still thrives.

The walls are thick with business cards — it's another custom to slap one on there after you've caught your buzz — and the urinal trough in the men's room carries a load of ice that's replenished throughout the afternoon. A guy in a seersucker suit rubs his eyes as he exits the restroom into the fray.

At the bar a Lucky Dog vendor in a candy-cane striped shirt who goes by the handle Shadowhawk keeps an eye out the window on his hot dog cart while he orders a beer. He's not from around here in the geographical sense — he came here about eight months ago, he says, just after the waters receded and they started to let people back in — but there's something about him that makes him fit in just fine with the street people of the French Quarter, something passionate and illogical and just a little bit insane.

"I don't know if you believe in spirits," he says, "but the spirit world called me here. I'm not here for the people, I'm here for the spirits."

Life is such at this place and moment in time that his declaration raises nary an eyebrow.

Goldie runs back and forth behind the bar. She's my friend and former bartending partner and host for the weekend (providing I'm willing to share the bed with a dog named Turkey and another one named Big).

It's good to see her. She, like everyone else who lived here before the flood, has her own tale of survival, evacuation, and exile: a few weeks spent on the Jersey shore with her boyfriend and the dogs before answering the undeniable pull of the city she's always called home.

She had a job within days; they're always looking for good bartenders in New Orleans, and Goldie has been practicing the craft since she was 14. Since then, it's been more or less life as usual for her down here.

We join with Atom and Nat'ly at NOLA, one of Emeril Lagasse's restaurants in the Quarter, and we eat six courses while mule-drawn carriages pass by the windows: an *amuse-bouche* of cold smoked salmon salad on butter crostini; a barbecue pork tortilla flavored with stout beer; a hanger steak with a cheese soufflé; a pan-fried crispy crab cake; stuffed Hoisin wings; barbecue shrimp with rosemary biscuits.

In between courses I run over to the bar to talk to Lori, a woman with whom I worked at a bar called Rosy's Big Easy back in 1991. It's been years since I've seen her.

"Yeah, I came back," she says. "I went to Sarasota and spent three days at the beach. I came back because my apartment didn't flood, because I couldn't find a job [in Florida]. I came back because I could, basically. But a lot of people are just gone. When you live in a disaster area you walk a fine line between denial and …"

She shrugs her shoulders. There is no flip side to denial.

———

The Isle of Denial. The Sliver by the River. The Bubble. That's what locals are calling the new New Orleans, the area that begins at the Uptown Riverbend and extends along the Mississippi to the French Quarter and into the Bywater, a stretch of high ground that sustained heavy damage from hurricanes Katrina and Rita but was not visited directly by the horrors of the flooding.

It's not completely unscathed — along Magazine Street many storefronts remain boarded or closed. Piles of garbage sit at intervals along the streets and power poles cant at odd angles. "Help Wanted" and "Now Hiring" signs hang in nearly every business. But you can still get a beer at nine in the morning, a great cup of coffee or an amazing meal at any time of day.

This is the part of New Orleans that most outsiders know: the Garden District; the Irish Channel; the streetcar line on St. Charles Avenue (which has ceased operation for the longest time since its first run in 1835); Loyola and Tulane universities; Audubon Park; the

Warehouse District; the Central Business District or, as the locals call it, the CBD; the French Quarter. And while it's easy to tell yourself that things are OK when you walk the streets or ride the bus lines, there have been some significant changes.

The rents, for one, have increased exponentially. When I lived there in the 1980s and '90s, you could find a nice one-bedroom apartment for about $500 a month. Now the same place might run $1,200 or $1,500 a month due to the vagaries of supply and demand.

And because for a period of time all the people in the city were forced to go elsewhere, the population has shifted and resettled. The deck of cards has been shuffled.

My friend Shawn, for instance, an infamous lower Decatur Street bartender, now works several miles away in the Uptown watering hole known as the Bulldog. Where she once wore tiny kilts to work and booked aggressive rock bands (a far, far cry from Bourbon Street Dixieland), these days she pours designer beers for starched-shirt yuppies and their girlfriends in this part of town that was once haunted by the St. Thomas Projects but is now a bit more like the Upper East Side.

Shawn lit out for Destin, Fla., a few days before the storm hit, she says. But like so many others, she felt the irresistible pull of the only place she's ever really lived. Her family is here. Her history is here. Her life is here, along with a house in Mid-City that made it out well, relatively speaking.

"I got homesick real bad," she says.

Shawn stayed gone six weeks.

My friend Pete, who has been working at the world famous Tipitina's for more than ten years, tells me his story in a few brief sentences as he cleans up the front bar after a hot show by three of the guys who make up the modern incarnation of the Meters, the city's most notorious funk band.

"I did ten days in Baton Rouge," he says. "We snuck back in

before they were letting people through. There was no way I wasn't coming back."

And at Igor's, the kind-of-shady, 24-hour Garden District watering hole where I worked the graveyard shift from 1995 until 2000, the song remains the same. Kerryn, the gun-toting Aussie expat, and her husband, Jerry, a former carny who to this day is the best storyteller I've ever known, work behind the bar together, making drinks for regular customers whom I still know by name: Tall Brian; Cox Cable Paulie, who no longer works for Cox but still answers to the name; Denise, who still gives tours of creepy locales in the Sliver; James, who will bus the front tables for a free draft beer. My picture is still on the wall, albeit a much younger and hairier version of myself, and they still keep the Jägermeister in the same place behind the bar.

The faux marble bar top has seen a coat of red paint since I've been gone, but other than that it's more or less exactly the way I left it six years ago.

And when I make it to the Balcony Bar on Magazine Street I see everybody from my old crew: Scottish Bryan, Pizza Guy Marc, Jan.

In the Isle of Denial, it seems to me anyway, there's quite a bit left of everything I remember.

The debris po-boy at Mother's on Poydras Street is a work of ingenuity. It's made from what's left over after the roast is cooked, the drippings and shreds of beef that collect in the bottom of the pan. It's paired with shredded cabbage — cheaper than head lettuce and with a longer shelf life — and loaded onto an airy hunk of French bread with Creole mustard, Blue Plate mayonnaise and whatever else they've got.

I've got one in front of me right now, the gravy seeping into the bread as I write these notes.

The line at the counter stretches to the back of the room this afternoon as it always has, and the service, still friendly to a fault, is slow enough to inspire hunger-induced anger and frustration in some of the out-of-town customers.

I took the Magazine bus down here to the CBD. The bus is free these days, one of the more pleasant unintended consequences of Katrina and the events that followed her, and I saw out the window the antiques stores, the bars, the restaurants that serve cheap and exotic food. I saw homes in states of repair, many clad in Tyvek home wrap with windows so new they still had the stickers on them.

It's the day of the mayoral runoff here in town and campaign signs share space with posted advertisements for mold removal, roof replacement, siding and insurance adjustment. Every lamppost, patch of grass and empty storefront has the ads, harbingers of the new economy.

The debris po-boy is the same as it ever was, a gooey, messy two-hander that will remind you that you ate it for the next few hours. I collect my things and begin a walk through the Quarter, my old neighborhood.

When I was something of a drunk I would cruise Decatur Street, the thoroughfare right along the river, until my pocketful of cash had depleted to nothing. Today I pick up Decatur on Canal Street, a block or so down from the casino, which is still doing a brisk business.

Decatur starts as a street of tourist traps off Canal and then gets progressively darker and more local as you head toward the Faubourg Marigny on the far side of the Quarter. At the beginning of my walk things seem much the same as I left them — the tourists still wear funny hats and obnoxious T-shirts, and drinkers avoid daylight in bars that have air-conditioning stripping instead of doors.

I duck into the Kerry, a tiny Irish bar near Canal, and run into Scottish Sharon, former girlfriend of Scottish Bryan. I haven't seen her in a long time.

Sharon made for Chicago after the flood but felt the pull of New Orleans within a few weeks. She's here now, she says, and she's considering a job offer in West Virginia. But she knows she'll be back with the same certainty she knows to mix a gin and tonic

At the House of Blues I find one of my best friends from my years down here, Chris, who had left years before I did but returned about three months before the flood.

He's been buying real estate since Katrina, he tells me, investment properties mostly. The bartending gig at the House of Blues is just a way to keep the cash moving. And he tells me he's not one of those landlords charging double or triple the pre-hurricane rate.

"If we jack people for whatever we can get," he says, "then we're not the kind of people we want to inhabit this city."

My walk continues down Decatur, past the Jax Brewery where a freight train rumbles by on the riverside tracks; past Jackson Square where the ranks of tarot card readers, sketch artists, and painted human statues have thinned a bit; past the bank of pay phones where once, on assignment for *Where Y'at Magazine,* I answered a ringing phone and was sexually solicited for my troubles by a guy watching me from another pay phone across the street.

I see that the Central Grocery, where the muffuletta sandwich was born, has closed, but my friend Maggie is back working at Molly's at the Market, and the Abbey is still the grossest bar in town.

I make a left on Governor Nichols Street and head back to my old bachelor pad on the corner of Burgundy — pronounced bur-GUN-dy — a third-floor walk-up with a wrought-iron balcony and the best view of the cityscape I've ever seen.

I look at my old balcony from the street, snap a few pictures, and then sit on the stoop where, on Memorial Day 1998, I found four menthol cigarette butts, an empty can of St. Ides malt liquor, and three human turds. As I sit I can almost convince myself that nothing's changed, that the last six years have been a dream and if I want I can turn around, go up the steps and out to my aerie, take in the view as the sun drops behind the Hibernia building, and watch the night people begin to take over the streets.

I enjoy the illusion for a moment. Then I move on.

The last time I saw Terry he was on TV having an emotional break-down.

"Yeah," he remembers, "MSNBC was in the car when I found out I got looted."

Terry is a lieutenant with the New Orleans Police Department, and he's recounting the scene on his mother's back deck while we eat cold shrimp remoulade.

Terry brought his own family's valuables to his mother's evacuated Uptown house, figuring they would be safe. But nothing was safe in the weeks following the flood. Though the depth of the water in this neighborhood only got to four feet or so, it was easy for looters to come in by boat, climb up the stairs, and make off with the goods.

The house is in great shape tonight, with deep colors, interesting furniture, and captivating works of art, though they've more or less given up maintaining the apartment on the first floor.

Terry's shaken off much of the trauma from after the storm: the desperate and disparate crowds with nothing left to call their own, the gangs of armed thugs roaming the streets, the robberies, the frenetic worries about his friends and family and the no-shows within the NOPD.

"Like two hundred people [on the force] were gone," he says. "That's a lot of people. A lot of them were just supposed to go and check on their wives and kids and stuff and they never came back.

"It was like being in a war zone," he continues. "We were working 'round the clock, hungry and dirty. I remember the fun stuff. We went and found a pool one night in a backyard and we took off our clothes and just bathed in the pool. And we're wet, naked, three guys, and here comes the helicopter with the big spotlight overhead. We just waved at it."

The indigenous sense of humor remains. Terry wears a T-shirt with the NOPD icon on the back. "Chocolate City Police" it reads.

And then underneath: "We're bitter."

His mother, a former artists' model and current private investigator named Webby, has made her version of stuffed crab for the main course, served *en casserole,* with roasted potatoes, and a vegetable dish of squash, onion and mint.

"And of course," Webby says, "buttah, buttah, buttah."

We clean our plates on the back deck with white noise coming in a rush from a fountain in the yard. At 8:15, when the sun goes down, the termites begin to swarm, and we hustle inside the house.

Later on tonight I'll head over to Le Bon Temps Roule on Magazine Street to reunite with my friends and see Joe Krown, one of the foremost organists left in the city, spin out a brand of funk that is unique to this part of the world. I'll dance and carry on (and come within a hair's breadth of getting smacked in the face).

The next afternoon I visit Loyola University, where I spent five years of my life, learned to write and to do my laundry, and was first introduced to the city of New Orleans. There are some new buildings, to be sure, but the benches in the student quad where we hung out are still there, and the Danna Center still smells the same.

I cross the street to Audubon Park and begin the walk to the far side. There are hundreds of people enjoying the day, biking and rollerblading, playing golf, having family reunions and crawfish boils under the live oaks. I'm looking for the Tree of Life, a gigantic oak where we used to hang out when I was in college and, if we were sober enough, climb up to the crotch more than 20 feet above the ground. I can't find it, but I do see a massive trunk that's been excavated from the ground and stripped of its limbs. I pray that I've lost my way and this is not the tree I've been looking for.

The park ends at Magazine Street and the grounds of the Audubon Zoo begin. I stay right and walk across the train tracks to the Fly, a grassy stretch along the Mississippi. It's the place where I used to play Ultimate Frisbee in college and boil crawfish as a young adult. It's the spot where I proposed to my wife with a scraggly handful of flowers and tears in my eyes.

And on this Sunday afternoon the Fly is alive and well. Summertime students sunbathe and frolic and the air smells like a mixture of beer, cayenne pepper, and the musk of the river as it rolls gently by. Jazz and hip hop pour from the stereos of cars with their doors propped open and more than a few kites soar through the air. If I wanted to, I could get in on a game of Frisbee with a group of guys out in the field.

In other words, it's business as usual.

The scene strikes me in a way that moves me to sit and jot a few notes.

"The people of New Orleans are going to be all right," I write. "The storm has passed; the cleanup has begun; and they do what it is they've always done in the face of adversity and seemingly insurmountable odds. They 'walk on gilded splinters.' They 'look ka pypy.' "'They went on down to the Audubon Zoo and they all axed for you.'"

I breathe in the smells of this peaceful, happy place. Then I flip my notebook closed and go on my way.

"The Lower Ninth," Allen tells me, "is the *coup de grâce.*"

Allen is my old professor, the man who wrangled me my first paid freelance gig. He's still a trusted advisor and friend. He's also still a working journalist who was one of the cadre of reporters who braved the aftermath to bring the story of a devastated New Orleans to the world.

"You could see the stars at night," he says of those first few weeks after the waters receded. "There weren't many birds, but you could see the helicopters."

After a meal of corn-fried oysters St. Charles, we get in his car and head to the Lower Ninth Ward.

During Hurricane Katrina, the eastern storm barricade gave way, sending a wall of water into the Lower Ninth. The entire neighborhood was under water, in some places more than ten feet.

Allen's taking me there now. I've got to see it to believe it, he tells me.

The houses are starting to look derelict. As we get closer to the canal, things get worse and worse. There are cars, hundreds of them, smashed from above, blasted from the side, flipped on their backs like helpless turtles, and all covered with a patina of milky residue.

And the houses, block after miserable block, have been tossed from their moorings; they've been crushed by the onrushing flood or wilted from standing water or pushed back from their stoops or outright collapsed from a combination of the insults heaped upon them. The ones still standing have the FEMA "X" spray-painted on the front, showing how many dead, the extent of the damage, the existence of toxic waters, whether or not any pets have been reported or spotted. It goes on like this for miles.

It's hard to describe. It's even harder to look at.

Allen stops the car. I gawk out the window. We're at Fats Domino's house in the neighborhood he's lived in all his life. It's a simple brick duplex with a black and gold roof piece, a neon sign, and his initials in big letters up there on the façade.

"They were dropping off flowers and stuff," Allen says. "People thought he was dead. There was all kinds of wild rumors flying around."

Fats was rescued by boat on the Monday after the storm and made it out OK. The house, especially when contrasted with the devastated neighborhood around it, looks good. And as far as anybody knows, Fats will be back. He's never lived anywhere else.

MAY 30, 2006

My Mardi Gras Memories Are Fuzzy

I'm writing this on Monday morning, pushing hard against a solid deadline. This is the way it's got to be. Because while in most of the world today is simply "Monday," down in New Orleans it's Lundi Gras, the chill-out period before the final blowout tomorrow, Fat Tuesday, Mardi Gras Day.

It's been five years since I took part in New Orleans' annual late winter bacchanal, five years of procreating, working, fixing my credit, and trying to bring my tolerance for alcohol, for which I once had an astounding capacity, down to a more respectable level.

Of course, Mardi Gras is not what it used to be — nothing down there is these days — but it gladdens my heart to see that they're still getting it on, still cavorting in the streets and nursing hangovers with Bloody Marys. It's nice to know you can still get a Zulu coconut or a long string of beads simply by exposing what the good lord gave you. And it gladdens my heart that you can still see tourists vomiting, peeing, or having sex in the street.

Peeing in the street, by the way, is still one of the more dangerous things one can do during Mardi Gras. Of everything I've mentioned, it's the only one that can land you in jail.

I know a little something about Mardi Gras — I've participated in no less than 13 of them, my first in 1989 when, as an 18-year-old college freshman, my mind was blown by the scenes of abandon I witnessed.

If you do Mardi Gras right, they say, you'll never be the same afterward. I know I never was. ...

By 1992, I was tending bar out on Tchoupitoulas Street, and by 1995, I was slinging drinks on St. Charles Avenue, the *grande dame* of Southern boulevards, where at Carnival time the parades roll by in barely interrupted threads. I made a good piece of money back then, and I held my own with drinkers from around the world. I have a store of memories that stand out in gauzy relief against the way my life is now. And it's true that I've certainly forgotten more than I recall.

But here are a few snippets that have survived the absolution of my life:

1989: I saw a detail cop in full New Orleans Police Department regalia in Fat Harry's with a beer in one hand and a college girl in the other. He paid equal attention to both.

1989: I saw my friend, the future salutatorian of a distinguished institution of higher learning, engaged in an act of coitus with an anonymous woman. On the hood of a car. At 4:30 in the afternoon.

1990: Again in Fat Harry's. On the Saturday before Fat Tuesday, the crowd got so thick that I was lifted off the beer-soaked floor by the pressure of the bodies around me. I was scared for my life and laughing at the same time.

1990: I shared my bottle of bourbon with a homeless guy on the street.

1991: My roommate found a bag of pills on the floor of a bar (probably Fat Harry's) and by experimentation and simple deduction we were able to discern what kind they were.

1992: After the parades, in a basement apartment off St. Charles, 11 guys in a room danced with reckless abandon for half an hour. "That was weird," one of us said when we were done.

1995: I worked a 19-hour shift at Qué Sera on St. Charles because nobody showed up to relieve me. By the time I was done at 4 a.m. my hands were shaking and I had about $600 in my pocket. It was barely worth it.

1996: Krazy Karl, a slightly overweight, tattooed, and pimpled metal head, cooked cheeseburgers naked behind my bar for the first time. It would become a Fat Tuesday tradition.

1997: I worked the door at Igor's, a 24-hour institution on St. Charles, on Fat Tuesday and slapped them all in the ass before I let them in.

1999: Jill and I found a stranger in our bed playing with our cat.

There's more: the woman who called herself "Earth Mama," who tried to sleep with every bartender on St. Charles before they cleaned the streets on Ash Wednesday; the passed-out cop who got hand-cuffed to the sink in the bathroom; the barely-clothed crowds of hipsters at the Mom's Ball; the costumed krewe of Jewlu and their party Tuesday morning at my boy Deuce's house before they stepped in behind the Zulu parade; the Mardi Gras Indians cruising Central City; the drum circle in the Bywater; the Widespread Panic fan who traveled with all his supplies in a tackle box. The rest of what I re-member is certainly unprintable, and you probably wouldn't believe me anyway.

It's just as well.

On Lundi Gras in Greensboro I'm drinking coffee and reminisc-ing to myself, more or less clearheaded. A call to my friend Brandon Carriveau in New Orleans assures me that they're still doing it, still partying even in the face of disaster, perhaps partying harder because of Katrina. Brandon says he's having one of his best Carnivals ever.

"It's been fucking awesome, man," he says. "I had to park seven blocks away."

Tomorrow morning at Igor's, the Bloodys will flow and the beads will fly just like they've always done. And when I drive by Interstate 40 today I'll say to myself, "What the hell … I can be there in 12 hours if I push it."

February 28, 2006

POSTCARD FROM NEW ORLEANS 2009

My wife and I left New Orleans nine years ago, before the flood-waters ravaged the city and its people. It's where we came of age, where we fell in love, where our first child was born. We're here to celebrate the nuptials of Atom and Nat'ly, who for a short time were Greensboro's favorite Katrina refugees. They went back to the Cres-cent City after about six months and now live in a modern cottage on the West Bank, which locals call the "Best Bank," both with and without irony.

We have other plans, too, of course. This is our city, and we plan to drink deeply from its chalice. We take our lodgings in the Uptown home of the former Webster St. Germain, three floors in the shot-gun style. Webby, a former artist's model, has covered the walls with artwork, and sculpture sits on every available surface. It takes days to catalog all the art, some of which depicts Web herself, clearly created by one of the men she has smitten in her life. Over the days, I count eight chandeliers hanging from the ceilings.

Uptown New Orleans was my haunt from 1988 until 1993, when I graduated from Loyola University — which still sits like a gem on the St. Charles streetcar line. Later I moved to the Garden District and then, thrillingly, to a back street in the French Quarter, the finest years of my youth.

On our first day in town, Jill and I hit some of the bars where I used to work. We have Bloody Marys at Madigan's on the Riverbend; we eat shucked oysters, crawfish pies, and shrimp po-boys at Cooter Brown's, where I worked the door as a 19-year-old, my first bar job.

We roll on the streetcar to the Garden District to Igor's, where I worked the graveyard shift from 1995 until 2000. Our pictures still adorn the wall of Igor's even all these years later, and there are a couple photos of our firstborn in the days after he was hatched. Scottish Brian is behind the bar and Brandi is out on the sidewalk. They have not forgotten us. Want to hear more about the food? We eat crawfish cheesecake and fried-oyster salad.

We drink beer made with fresh strawberries from Ponchatoula and many cups of good coffee. I devour the greatest roast beef po-boy in the world at Parasol's, my friend Jeff's Irish Channel bar; and at Jacques-Imo's I take down another roast beef po-boy, this one soaked in gravy, dipped in batter, and deep fried. I eat the whole thing with a knife and fork. The night before the wedding, Atom cooks a *Fowl de Cochon,* which is a chicken stuffed inside a duck stuffed inside a turkey stuffed inside a suckling pig. As for music, we catch the Tin Men at d.b.a. down in the Marigny, Kermit Ruffins blowing his horn at Vaughan's in the Ninth Ward while Walter "Wolfman" Washington sits at the bar and taps his feet. (He later sits in with some mesmerizing licks.) We wander into the Maple Leaf on Oak Street and find Robert Mercurio and Jeff Raines of Galactic holding court on the stage and my old editor from *Where Y'at Magazine* tending bar. The cover charge: four bucks.

The entire city of New Orleans is a work of art. But the greatest thing about it, I believe, are the beautiful people who live there. Jill and I may have forgotten how many friends we have down there, but we are reminded within minutes of touching down: José and the Doc, Georgie Boy and Jen, Tremmell and Big Tiny, Mark and Myron, Gutshot Steve, Newcastle Dave (who made the trip in from San Francisco after leaving New Orleans five years ago), Big Bald Glen, F&M Deb, Jeremy, Jan, and Scottish Sharon ... and on and on.

The wedding goes down in the rose garden at City Park, which is tranquil and serene, surrounded by blooms. In the pond sits a vaguely pornographic sculpture of a woman riding a dolphin among the lily pads, and red-throated geckos scamper along the shrubbery.

Bruce Daigrepont and his band play a slow Cajun waltz. Atom and Nat'ly, newly married, blissful, step and turn, step and turn. The clouds hang low in the blue, blue sky, and a balmy breeze ruffles the fronds of the date palms. We drink to the bride and groom. We smell the sweet air. We laugh and we love. We are in New Orleans, and everything is right.

APRIL 15, 2009

Ghosts of Football Seasons Past

The City of New Orleans and the Saints are one and the same. The Saints are the rice in the gumbo, the lemon peel in the Sazerac — or, if you prefer, the cucumber in the Pimm's Cup.

It's bigger than that, actually. The Saints are more than just a football team. And New Orleans is more than just a city.

Much has been made in the weeks leading up to Super Bowl XLIV of the symbiotic relationship between the people of New Orleans and the Saints, the football team they love. And I'm here to tell you it is real, a palpable bond that has endured decades of losing seasons, squandered leads, dropped passes, and unwise draft choices. Saints fans never cared if their team won a Super Bowl. And when we finally got to the Bowl, we decided there would be a celebration regardless of the outcome.

And so it was that I watched cornerback Tracy Porter's game-changing, fourth-quarter interception with Linda Morphis of Hattiesburg, Miss., a lifelong Saints fan who has been tuning in on Sunday afternoons since 1967, when John Gilliam ran back the very first opening kick against the Los Angeles Rams in Tulane Stadium.

"After church," she said, "we'd all come home and watch the Saints."

We were at her son Emmett's house, drinking Abita beer, she in her Who Dat sweatshirt and me with a *fleur de lis* stenciled on my neck. We never thought we'd see the day.

And while black and gold confetti rained down upon Sun Life Stadium in Miami, my thoughts turned to New Orleans and my own experience with the Saints, a torrid love affair that began quickly and has never ended.

I went to nearly every home game between 1995 and 2000, heading to the Superdome after ending my bar shift at about 10 a.m., usually with my friend Ray, who held season tickets near the end zone.

Ray was a bar customer — one of my best. He could put away vodka and Sprites at a pace that, even by New Orleans standards, was impressive. He was an engineer who worked in one of the city's shipyards designing systems for the gigantic vessels that navigated down to the mouth of the Mississippi River and into the Gulf of Mexico. He was the first visitor in the hospital when my oldest son was born, and the most generous gifter at my wedding. And he was a low-key homosexual who once confided in me that he had absolutely no sexual interest in women.

"I've tried it," he said. "It just doesn't do it for me." Whatever. I've never really concerned myself with the ways other adults like to achieve orgasm.

But Ray and I would hit the Superdome hard on Sunday afternoons, knocking back Bloody Marys in the upstairs bar, screaming ourselves hoarse, dancing to the music until the cameraman would project us onto the Diamond Vision screen high above the field. Then we'd cruise the French Quarter looking for sexual conquests — that is, until I met the woman who would become my wife and Ray met Sammy, a hairdresser from Baton Rouge, La., who captured his heart in a way that no woman ever could.

I thought of Ray a lot during this miracle Saints season, particularly when CBS declined to air a commercial for a gay dating website called ManCrunch. Here's a bit of news: Lots of gay guys like football. Some of them even play it professionally.

I wish I could have called Ray, but he's gone — died five years ago, the morning my daughter was born. It's likely he drank himself to death, something for which I am at least partially responsible.

Those vodka Sprites didn't pour themselves.

A lot of the old guys from the bar have moved on from this world: Roger the Dodger, Old Rick, Navy Dave — Saints fans one and all.

They're joined by a horde of Who Dats who couldn't hang on long enough to witness this miracle in Miami performed by the only Saints who mattered on football Sunday afternoons. But down in New Orleans, where spirits seem to linger far longer than they do in other places, I am sure they know what went down this weekend. And the ones who lived through the thrill were surely doing their part to raise the dead.

I'm sure Ray heard the fracas emanating from the French Quarter, and Roger the Dodger and Old Rick and all the rest did, too. I can picture them out there in the ether, arguing about statistics, second-guessing play calls, and gesturing for more rounds of drinks. While I don't wish I were sitting beside them, I sure do miss them. And I would have loved to have seen their faces as the game clock wound down to zero and the Saints became champions of the world.

FEBRUARY 12, 2010

Poverty and Poundage
in the Caribbean

I'm on the 14th deck of the Royal Caribbean Mariner of the Seas, some 180 feet above sea level, though the big blue is all around me, far and wide, its surface glittering like it's been speckled with polished yellow diamonds. A rim of thick glass windows encircles Ellington's Martini Bar, and from where I'm sitting I believe I can discern the curve of the earth.

It's our seventh day aboard, and you might think we'd be accustomed to the grandeur, the opulence, the sheer enormity of the vessel.

We're not.

It's a behemoth. A titan. The newest and largest ship in the line. And though I've caught just about every episode of "The Love Boat," I've never seen anything like this before.

There are a slew of restaurants, shops, and bars on board. Theaters, swimming pools, hot tubs, and lounges. There is a rock-climbing wall, a mini-golf course, a basketball court, a casino, a nightclub, and an in-line skating rink. There is Bingo and karaoke and trivia and dancing. Every morning a breakfast expanse awaits, and every evening our cabin attendant makes delightful animals from rolled towels. Last night we had a stingray stretched across our bed; the night before, a terry-cloth monkey hung from a coat hanger.

We are living like veal, with free and abundant food around every corner; helpful and eager valets with easy smiles and a directive to please; a soft bed; a grand cabin; and a thousand little places to sit, eat, drink, or schmooze.

There are 3,300 passengers aboard, and more than a thousand crew — a greater population than the university I attended. The occasion is a seven-day Caribbean jaunt for employees of an encapsulated herb company with which my wife enjoys association. They're from all over the United States, with a healthy contingent of Utah Mormons, and a near majority of middle-class Latinos. Also on board: a smattering of Amish and Mennonites who seemed cowed by the luxury the first few days. Now, the bearded men wear bright island shirts with their staid trousers and suspenders. The women have not strayed from their bonnets and ankle-length skirts, even in these tropical climes.

Our first port of call was Haiti on Tuesday — a part of the island owned, apparently, by the cruise line. We made land on an open-decked tender and took in the coarse-sand beaches, the poverty-stricken islanders peddling identical wares in an aggressive manner, the sunburned and swollen *turistas* plodding through this facsimile of paradise.

Most of them didn't notice the high black fence separating the beach from the jungle, meant to keep the poverty and disease of one of the poorest and least stable nations in its rightful place.

We noticed.

As we looked at the fence, a young man slithered down from the jungle canopy and traversed a steep and rocky slope to speak to us in low tones.

"We are very poor," he said.

I crumpled a dollar in my fist and approached the fence, and the man implored me to climb over. I did not, but I tossed the bill over, and he scampered to pocket it.

"I will pray for your whole family," he said.

As we walked back to our idyll, several more bodies materialized from the bush and joined our man in silent retreat.

The dissonance between our luxury liner and our island hosts was apparent also in Jamaica, where we successfully eluded the strong-arm tour guides at the dock, only to be ... kidnapped? ... by a Rastafarian cab driver named Cool Marco who took us through the hills of Ocho Rios, where natives alternately waved and smiled at us or glared through heavy-lidded, red-rimmed eyes. Cool Marco even took us to his house in the green, green hills, in a place he called "Hand to Mouth Street," and showed us the fruits and herbs on his property that have sustained his family for generations.

He was pleasant and good-natured, but the desolation of the dirt-paved neighborhood, the heavy glances from locals, and the discovery of a long-handled knife in the front seat of Cool Marco's cab made for a terrifying experience.

They say travel is an investment in one's self, and this is an *a priori* truth. This trip has included many firsts for me: my first time in the islands, my first vacation away from my kids, my first cruise. It's also the farthest away from New York, the place I grew up, that I have been. And the experience, I can say, has been dynamite for my psyche, blasting away the coagulating stresses of family and work and clearing my neural pathways for the challenges that lie waiting in the months ahead, like starving Haitians lurking in the hardwoods.

Tomorrow we make land in the more saccharine environs of Orlando, where we'll board a plane and then be reunited with our children, whom we miss almost more than we can bear, and with our regular lives, which don't seem as oppressive as they did just a week ago. Things will be, as they say, "back to normal." But for my wife and me, these poles of opulence and squalor will remain fixed in our memory, even as we struggle to work off the poundage we've acquired from all the midnight buffets.

JUNE 7, 2007

OUR MAN IN CANNES

"Innndeeeeeeee!"

"Iiiinnnnnn Deeeeeeeeee!"

"INNNNNNNDEEDEEEEEEEEEE"

The crowd is going straight-up bananas outside the *Palais des Festivals,* the red-carpeted stairs rising behind them like some whorish Aztecan pyramid.

"Innnndeeeee."

It's Sunday, the fifth day of *le Festival de Cannes,* and the Boulevard de la Croisette has already seen thousands of tourists, dozens of red-carpet strolls, and the somewhat disturbing spectacle of a karate-chopping Jack Black in front of a cadre of big, fat pandas. Today there are free Indiana Jones hats for anyone with elbows sharp enough to wedge through the crowd and exclamations loud enough to catch the attention of the promotional hotties in cargo shorts — a blonde and a tanned brunette — both in Indy hats themselves.

"INNNDEEE!," they scream from behind the police barricades as the hotties pass to the loudest those cheap brown fedoras, each emblazoned with the fiery logo from Dr. Jones' newest adventure, *Indiana Jones and the Kingdom of the Crystal Skull,* starring a somewhat wizened Harrison Ford, who today ascended the red carpet with Steven Spielberg and Cate Blanchett in tow, to the snapping of a thousand shutters.

It's probably the most notorious film of the 2008 festival — the highest budget, the biggest stars, the largest promotional presence in billboards and banners along the Croisette — and there's serious kinetic action down here on the sidewalk among the hooples, pretty much all of whom will have to get in line and buy a ticket if they want to catch the on-screen action. But for now, there's always the hats.

"Innndeee!"

And now everybody's wearing them, from the stroller-pushing weekend tourists to the drunken, slumming cosmopolitans to the bleary-eyed paparazzi standing on ladders under the date palm trees, with clear sightlines to the red carpet. And by the main entrance to the *Palais des Festivals,* several floors removed from the aerie described by those crimson stairs but certainly more accessible to us regular folk, the buzz is strong for this film, which comes nearly 20 years after the last installment of the series.

"Indee!" fancy locals say as they hold up signs begging for tickets, accented with the letters "SVP," which I've come to understand means *si'l vous plait.*

"Indee!" say the slick-ass tuxedoed Euroboys as they hold up a homemade banner bearing an interpretation of the film's logo.

"Indy!" they say as they pose for pictures in their cheap brown fedoras and bought-for-the-occasion shades, sunburns settling into their forearms and the backs of their necks.

And for this moment the buzz over Spielberg's newest blockbuster runs like a current through this part of the Croisette, and you might start to think to yourself, God damn, son, I gotta go see this movie.

But the word among the insiders, those with super-sharp tuxedos and jewels that twinkle like personal celestialities and small decks of laminates slung around their necks like VIP tarot, the ones whose opinions matter at this moment more than that of anyone who might eventually see the film, has already been spoken, and now it lays there like an epitaph, indelible and forever.

Indiana Jones and the Kingdom of the Crystal Skull kind of sucks.

This is the 61st *Festival de Cannes,* the most famous film festival in the world. It was born in the cradle of fascism and, in fact, owes its existence to those brown- and black-shirts who dared to place politics over art.

Before Cannes, the largest film festival was the Venice Film Festival, its top prize, no shit, called the Mussolini Cup. In 1938 Jean Renoir's *La Grande Illusion* lost to what many consider to be a Nazi propaganda film, Leni Riefenstahl's *Olympia,* which was financed by German Minister of Propaganda Joseph Goebbels.

The French weren't having it. In 1939, *Le Festival International du Film* was born in Cannes, but Nazi Germany's invasion of Poland preempted it.

Over the years, the festival has generated its own historical footnotes: Brigitte Bardot was discovered posing topless for photographers on the beach one year, in the days before celebrity sex tapes introduced us to up-and-coming talent. Grace Kelly met Prince Rainier here, the first chapter of their international love story. An unfinished version of *Apocalypse Now* won the *Palme d'Or,* the festival's highest prize, in 1979.

The list of films that have won the festival's top prize is astounding. It includes *La Dolce Vita; M*A*S*H; Taxi Driver; All That Jazz; Paris, Texas; The Pianist; Fahrenheit 9/11.*

By now, you're probably asking yourself what a two-bit journalist from the North Carolina Triad is doing here, notebook in hand, rubbing elbows and hustling party invites with filmdom's elite.

It's a fair question. And the short answer is: I cheated.

I am not a filmmaker. Except, in another, more accurate sense, I am. My journey to Cannes began last August as part of a crew that entered the Greensboro leg of the international 48 Hour Film Project, wherein a five- to seven-minute film must be written, shot, and edited in the span of two days. We came up with *JoBeth,* the sparse tale of a sad, abused girl who is trying to make a break from her horrible life. And after a hectic shoot, we ended up winning in Greensboro. A couple of months later, at the project's finale, Filmapalooza in San Jose, Calif., we were named in the top dozen out of a couple thousand international entrants. With the honor came the opportunity to screen in the Short Film Corner in the basement of the *Palais des Festivals* during the festivities in Cannes. A few months of preparation and fundraising, and here I am strolling the Croisette in this mad, beautiful throng. The only difference between them and me is that most people screening films at the festival worked half a lifetime to get here; the work that brought me here, my individual contribution, took about five hours.

There are five of us from the crew and we've secured a small villa up in the hills of Le Cannet overlooking the beachfront city. We've got five days, a modest bankroll by Cannes standards — the dollar is running about two to one against the euro — and low-level passes that give us access to the *Palais des Festivals,* hulking like a giant brick on the beach, to the Short Film Corner, and little else. No matter to a guy like me. I've always been able to survive pretty well by my wits, and every journalist knows it's easier to get forgiven than it is to get permission. Besides, unless you're a high-level industry insider, an up-and-coming starlet willing to put out, or the owner of a mega-yacht docked on the pier, all the action is in the bars and on the streets.

My mandate is simple: experience, experience, experience. Talk to as many people as possible; have some great meals; drink with the locals and run with the tourists; keep an eye out for celebrities; keep an ear to the ground. And most of all, see if I can sweet-talk this magnificent city and this spectacular festival to yield some of their secrets to me.

The first 48 hours go by in a frenetic blur.

Our crew assembles by the *Palais,* we secure our credentials, and, after I sneak into a reception at the Short Film Corner, which I was not entitled to attend — "How did you get in here?" a woman from

New York asked me — we take dinner at a side street café with other filmmakers from the 48 Hour Film Project.

We walk the seaside streets for awhile, through beautiful neighborhoods overlooked by wrought-iron balconies and balustrades, and then head back to the villa to put on nighttime clothes: black suits and gowns; hard, shiny shoes.

By then we've met up with a local by the name of Michael who's been cruising the hills on a ballsy scooter. After we hit a beachside tent party featuring 20-dollar drinks and lingeried hotties who wriggle on tabletops, we ask him to take us to a cool bar. He leads us down a short side street to a nightspot called Sun 7, which is where we ushered in the dawn every night thereafter.

On that first night I meet a phalanx of Brits, one of whom leads the kind of life I would have sworn I'd be living if you would have asked me 20 years ago. He is wealthy, international, single, and rich. Plus he's huge, with a head like a magnificent pumpkin and an ass that looks like it was made from cinderblocks. I take to calling him "Big Me."

His friend, who in his white bow tie looks like a symphony conductor, is interested in our path to Cannes. He asks me what I'm working on, and I synopse the plot of a novel I've been kicking around for a few years. I tell him my major apprehension about screenwriting: that it is stripped of the little details and stylistic prose that I've come to see as aspects of my overall style.

Back at Sun 7 the next night I see him again.

"I've been thinking about your screenplay," he tells me. "You know, in Eastern Europe, scripts come in two parts. The first is a description, kind of like a novel. The second consists of only dialogue. Just lines. I think perhaps you might be more comfortable with that style."

I think: Perhaps I would.

Like any good American during his first time abroad, I become filled with a sense of patronizing acceptance of my nation and countrymen.

Their money makes so much sense, I think. Different colors and sizes. And two-euro coins? That's pure genius. I've got a pocketful of change and it's like 20 bucks.

Two different flushes on the toilets? A small one for a piss and a big one for a crap? Brilliant! Why can't we do that?

"How does it feel to live in a poor country?" we ask each other every time we exchange dollars for euros.

And: "You would never see that in the States," we say, rarely in a positive light.

It is an easy thing to be seduced by Cannes, particularly during the festival when you're carousing down a street closed in by ancient architecture, surrounded by beautiful people from the finer corners of the world, a steady parade of six-figure cars rolling slowly, conspicuously by.

But even at its bones the city is remarkable, an amalgamation of U.S. cities that I love the most. It has the climate of San Francisco and its geography, too, with craggy, cave-dotted shores. There are palisades like those upriver from Manhattan, and, of course, there are echoes of New Orleans' French Quarter, my old neighborhood, everywhere I look.

In all my encounters, I experience not a shred of anti-American sentiment. Most Frenchmen I meet seem to feel sorry for us, and three of them, on separate occasions, bring up 9/11 and the collapse of the Twin Towers. They do so reverently, almost apologetically. "We do not understand why," one man at a café told me.

Michael, the scooter-riding local, leaves a bag of fresh cherries on our doorstep the day after taking us around town. And on my second day, when I get off at the wrong bus stop on my way up to Le Cannet, a middle-aged French couple pulls out a map and drives me to the doorstep of my villa.

The scenery is magnificent, the food, sublime. There are no mosquitoes and the air smells fresh and sweet, save for the occasional whiff of alcohol vapors that seem to be coming from the scooters everyone maneuvers through traffic.

And when I ponder this society they've built here on the banks of the Mediterranean, I keep thinking about something pundit Chris Matthews said on television one night when describing another European nation.

"Do you ever get the feeling they're playing chess and we're playing checkers?"

On Tuesday night at *le Petit Majestic,* the waiter, a fellow who looks to be in his 40s, wears horn-rimmed glasses, earring plugs that blink colored lights, a mesh T-shirt, booty shorts that highlight his package, black thigh-high stockings with a pack of Marlboros tucked into them, and a pair of Puma high-tops in metallic green. And he's pulling it off.

We'd heard about this place the night before — it's the unofficial Riviera clubhouse of the British film industry — but couldn't even get near it and settled in at Sun 7 to usher in the morning.

But we're here tonight, and the fancy waiter has already propositioned me.

"Twenty-three euros," he says, and then prances over to a waiting cab, gesturing to me wildly.

I am unsure of local customs and therefore don't know which one of us is on the paying end of the transaction, and, damn it, if I were gay I just might give this guy a go. But no matter how many pastis the guy sells me, it is just not gonna happen for him.

Ah yes, the pastis ... a little bombshell I discover quite by accident, tipped off by a passing fancyman holding a cloudy glass of the stuff. It's a gentler version of absinthe, stripped of wormwood when that vile stuff became banned. The liqueur, which when diluted with water is likely the most popular drink in the country, still packs quite a wallop, and I may even mean it when I say I am never drinking that shit again.

The night was still a winner, though. We hooked up with a

Finnish crowd who had procured a small apartment overlooking Rue d'Antibes, just above a Dolce & Gabbana retailer. There, on a rooftop patio amid lemon trees and a gently falling rain, we sipped a Finnish beer called Koff and watched their trailers. One was for a feature called *Iron Sky,* a sci-fi comedy about a Nazi colony established on the dark side of the moon in 1948 which is now preparing to invade Earth.

You kind of had to be there.

And in the street outside *le Petit Majestic,* while I'm standing there gabbing on about god knows what, I turn around and literally rub elbows with Spielberg as he passes through the crowd. He was so close I could have stolen his watch.

At least I think it was him. Pastis, you know.

I may very well be the only North Carolina-based journalist in Cannes for this year's festival. I was turned down for press credentials, a fact that the festival keepers actually had on record, which I discovered when I tried to bullshit my way into a temporary press cred.

But more than 4,000 members of the press are here, from more than 1,600 media outlets, television and print, mostly. The *Los Angeles Times* has a banner hanging from a hotel balcony and *Variety* has established a beachhead in a small strip behind the Grand Hotel where its staffers file their stories in a newsroom that an editor tells me is "private" just before bouncing me out.

And over on the patio at the Grand Hotel the journos ease in for afternoon drinks and late deadlines. A table of television folk prepare for a six-o'clock package to air in the United States; a fellow laptop rattler sips a cocktail at a table on the grass and searches for that perfect word. And still, just down the lawn, the Croisette flows like a vital artery.

The paparazzi move hurriedly in small packs, many wearing rumpled and sweaty tuxedoes but others looking appropriately unprofessional. Or they gather in flocks, perched on ladders like birds on a wire, craning for that perfect shot. Or they pick a spot and wait out their prey, like those TMZ guys camped out on the docks under the tent outside Diddy's yacht. Or they hunt alone, picking out famous faces who have strayed from the VIP rooms, from behind the velvet ropes. They drop to a knee and start shooting right there in the street. And invariably, within seconds, they are joined by fellow solitary hunters.

Perhaps in different surroundings it would seem distasteful. But no one in Cannes is here to be ignored, and the ability to attract attention is a prized talent. In fact, this is what showbiz is all about: to be able to yell, "Hey everybody, look over here!" and get people to pay attention to what you're doing, hold them there for a meaningful amount of time.

This comes to me in a pastis-induced epiphany, which was inspired by an event earlier in the day.

Down in the film market in the main chamber beneath the *Palais,* we happen upon a trailer for a film called *Ong-Bak 2* starring a guy named Tony Jaa. Jaa is the baddest, quickest, most creative martial-arts ass kicker I've ever seen on film. An example: In one scene he grabs a guys Adam's apple, twists it upside down, and then cocks it like a shotgun.

We sit and watch for a while, and pretty soon a crowd gathers, and we're all like, "Ooooh!" and, "Awwwwww!" and "Daaaamm-mmm!"

Before the trailer runs its course, a guy with a sweater tied around his neck who stinks like money approaches, waving a business card in his hand and speaking in a British accent.

"Who is selling this film?"

It's all about the eyeballs.

JUNE 30, 2008

PART 4

STRONG ISLAND

Class Reunion Train Wrecks

The friend requests have been tumbling in for weeks on my Facebook page, reaching critical mass this weekend with a final crush of long, lost faces.

I'm also getting Snapfish alerts and text messages, and my image is likely being tagged somewhere even at this moment. The precipitating event was my high school reunion, from which, as of this afternoon, I am still recovering. The event took place Saturday night up on Long Island, where more than 150 members of the Garden City High School Class of 1988 gathered to see how old everybody had gotten.

There's more to it than that, of course. My high school was kind of an insular institution. We didn't often socialize with students from other high schools, and because we lived in a place and time where neighborhoods had more consistency, we all knew each other fairly well. I knew all the names of the 350 students in my graduating class. At least I did when I was a high school student. The night of the reunion, huddled around the kitchen table at Espo's house, paging through our yearbook, there were dozens of people I had forgotten.

Our small pre-reunion crew included guys I have known since kindergarten, some of whom I hadn't laid eyes on in at least ten years. We were in the same classes, took the same field trips, played on the same soccer teams, and ate lunch at each other's houses back when we took a school bus home for lunch every day.

There we were — Roller, Carter, Espo, Hoolie, Joseph, Morano, Dr. Lawyer, and I — flipping through the pages and playing a game called Dark Horse. Without getting into too many details, it involved a bit of handicapping as to who had best weathered the last 20 years, with special attention paid to the women of the class. It turned out to be an exercise in futility. Virtually every member of the Class of 1988 who attended the reception looked fantastic, and many of them looked exactly as they did the year *Appetite for Destruction* came out. It was something, all right.

Just about half of our class made it to the reunion. We schmoozed while music from our teenage years played. We sampled liberally from the open bar and ignored the buffet that sat in the corner like a wallflower. A large screen flashed snapshots from the days when we were young: cat's-eye sunglasses, acid-wash jeans, big hair, and all. Homecoming. The Spring Fling. Spirit Day. The hundreds of house parties and gatherings where we cemented our bonds and drank ourselves silly on Meister Brau and Rheingold and the short-lived phenomenon that was the wine cooler.

It all seemed so harmless back then, but the bottle has affected more than a few of my classmates and their families.

But this space today is for happier feelings, so let me tell you who I saw: the kid who lived across the street who became my partner in crime for much of the '70s and '80s; the guy I got busted with in the high school parking lot doing … something we shouldn't have been doing; the dude I went through school with from kindergarten all the way through college; the owner of the very first pair of breasts I ever fondled. I saw all the guys I still keep in touch with but whom I don't get to see enough. And dozens and dozens of others who shared my youth, a youth that was not wasted but was … taken lightly.

For a lot of my current friends, high school was something of a nightmare. But I had a lot of fun in those days, largely because of the people in that room Saturday night.

We drank and circulated, told our stories, and caught up on recent news. We laughed at our teenaged selves even as we felt, for a few hours, like we were still in high school. And we marked a milestone as a group: 20 years gone, and we're still at it.

As for the game called Dark Horse, I'm afraid the jury's still out. There are a lot of photos to comb through, some Facebook footage to be vetted, and some memories to be plumbed before we can assign a winner.

OCTOBER 1, 2008

SAVING A FRIEND
AND A PIECE OF MY PAST

I step out of the baggage claim and into the February gray. The bitter wind makes my nose run, makes my eyes water. I fumble for my matches and curse the cold.

I hate New York in February.

I got the call yesterday afternoon. The news wasn't good. Cap, from the old neighborhood ... he's in a tailspin. Locked in his apartment for the last six weeks. Drinking Scotch by the bucketful. Lost his job. Lost everything. And quite possibly dying.

I got him on the phone. He didn't deny it. I asked him what he was doing to himself.

"It's horrifying," he said.

I got on a plane at six the next morning. And now here I am ... back in New York ... trying to help my boy before I have to bury him.

Dr. Lawyer picks me up from LaGuardia. It's good to see him.

Cap, Dr. Lawyer, and I go way back, to the point where we can't remember ever not knowing each other. We became young inebriates together back when our flesh was still pink, our psyches raw and burgeoning. We've been through countless good times and unspeakably bad ones. We're brothers. And it's only right that Dr. Lawyer and I take the trip to the Upper East Side. Cap's not listening to anybody else.

And we're not so sure he'll listen to us.

I make the call to him from his stoop on East 81st Street.

"Cap. It's Clarey. I'm outside. Buzz me in. It's goddamn freezing out here."

Miraculously, he buzzes the door open without argument or hesitation. Dr. Lawyer and I climb to the sixth floor of the walkup. Cap's waiting for us at the door of his apartment. He lets us in.

"Welcome to hell," he says.

It's a junkie's pad, a Manhattan hovel about half the size of my garage — empty, grimy walls and random stacks of clutter on the floor. Cap's slung a greasy, stained futon over his threadbare couch, about three feet from the TV against the other wall. There are cigarette butts in the toilet and another collection atop a pile of dirty plates in the kitchen. The window is broken. In one corner a naked mattress sags deeply through the middle, collecting a sweaty puddle of sheets. In another stand eight one-gallon Scotch bottles, the kind with the handle. They're empty.

Cap says he's been drinking one of these a day. He's got a cocktail going right now in fact, a mugful of undiluted amber spirit sitting on the folding chair he's been using as an end table.

In his closet hangs a row of neglected Italian suits and pressed shirts.

"I can't believe you came up from North Carolina," he says. His eyes are wet.

He's shirtless and I can see how his once athletic body has atrophied to flab. His ancient jeans are blown out at the knees and there's thick goop blocking his tear ducts and collecting in the corners of his mouth.

Cap can't believe his eyes either. He didn't think anybody cared.

He makes me take off my hat and tells me I look like Sean Lennon. It's not intended as a compliment. That's a good sign.

"We're gonna get you out of here," Dr. Lawyer says.

"I can't believe you guys are here," Cap says again. He finds a blue shirt and buttons it halfway up. He slips a defeated pair of sneakers over his filthy socks. He collapses into our arms, fear, grief, and relief overwhelming him at the tail end of his binge.

He has trouble walking down the stairs.

"He's got edema in his legs," Dr. Lawyer had said over the phone. He also warned of liver damage and encephalitis, and he thumbnailed the excruciating process of drying out at this stage of the game. He said Cap's been rehabbed more than a dozen times in the last two years, in every hospital in Manhattan. Once he had received an Ativan drip so potent that it raised the eyebrows of anyone who knew what the hell he was talking about. Still, Cap always managed to get himself out after a couple of days.

We hope this time will be different. Dr. Lawyer says it might.

On the city sidewalk I've got my arm around Cap's shoulders. We make ungainly progress to Dr. Lawyer's car. I let him sit in the front, and he laboriously climbs in. We pull away from the curb and Cap spins around, a wide smile on his face, and he bounces slightly in his seat like he always used to do,

"So where we going guys?

We're in high school again, cruising the streets of our hometown, looking for parties, for people, for action, logging the kinds of hours that make people friends for life.

Then Dr. Lawyer steers the car to the Triborough Bridge and the congested arteries that lead back to Long Island.

We're going home.

FEBRUARY 21, 2006

Roots

I'm traveling westbound on a West End bus through Long Beach, N.Y., wedged in a seat between a weekend's worth of groceries in white plastic bags and a deeply tanned local who looks to be about 60 and smells of gin, cigarettes and surf, with a healthy dose of human filth thrown in to the aromatic cocktail as well.

We're moving down Beech Street, past shirtless kids on skateboards and old ladies in big sunglasses, past streets named for states and sidewalks, named for months, which cut through the city blocks. I'm traveling through time, as well — at least in my mind, which has been amped up with coffee and then blasted with sense memory until I start thinking like the teenager I used to be when I ran around these streets in the summers of my youth.

Here's the asphalt baseball diamond, where sliding into third base was a risky proposition, to say the least. There's the site of the surf shop where I bought my first wetsuit. And that's the place that used to be Angelo's, at least I think it is, where Angelo himself used to mix egg creams behind the soda counter. He called them "salubrious egg creams."

"You know what salubrious means?" he'd ask. "It means horious. You know what horious means? Salubrious." I have since learned what salubrious means, and that egg creams — which contain no eggs at all but are drinks made from milk, chocolate syrup, seltzer, and whipped cream — are anything but. I also now know that "horious" is a word that Angelo made up.

Today on the bus I sit across from a Long Beach brother, a crazy one with headphones around his neck and wearing a black cowboy hat that has seen better days. Around the brim he's affixed tiny cowboy figurines on horseback and also a large silver cutout of what looks to be a Colt .45. He's talking to the driver about guns.

"When you can pick off a squirrel running," he says, "you know you're good with a pistol."

"I heard that," the driver says.

Then they start talking about knives, particularly the blade wielded by Sylvester Stallone in the *First Blood* series of action films, the one with the serrated edge and a compass screwed into the handle.

At the end of the line I dismount and make for the Atlantic Beach Club. I smoke a cigarette on the way, a habit I picked up at an inappropriately young age in the tiny video game parlor at the front of Angelo's and perfected in the grassy dunes on either side of the club.

There are no crazy brothers at ABC — no brothers at all, in fact, though there are plenty of deep, dark skin tones courtesy of baby oil and cocoa butter, lots of sun-bleached hair and kids with freckles and sun-burnt shoulders, lots of pricey bathing suits, lots of women with personal trainers and guys who make seven figures but spend their summers in cabanas smaller than my first apartment.

It's a New York stronghold of the privileged and elite against the unpleasantness of the real world, where they can enjoy the sand and sea without being reminded that there are people in this town who don't earn as much in a year as their seasonal bar tabs, tennis fees, and bathing suit allowances.

I've been coming here since I was five — for 30 summers — and I owe as much to this place as I do to the cracked sidewalks and crowded streets of Long Beach. I swam and surfed in the ocean here, skinned my knees on the club's concrete pool deck, and got splinters in my feet from its wooden boardwalks. I played manhunt and ringolevio in the dunes and did can-openers off the high dive (which, for insurance reasons, no longer exists). I learned a two-handed backhand on the tennis courts and, when I got a bit older, became schooled in the ways of the drink.

Jeff the bartender makes Bloody Marys with clam juice and a reasonable dose of horseradish, and even though I am a once-a-year customer he fixes me one when he sees me walk through the door. The bar is empty on this Saturday afternoon, save for me and Jeff. Out the big windows I can see a stretch of fine, clean sand dotted with umbrellas and furniture that folds, and also the expanse of the Atlantic Ocean, which stretches to the horizon and never fails to bring me peace, if only for a moment.

Tonight there'll be fireworks, which will dazzle my children as they once did me, exploding in the New York sky as we watch on the sand below. I'll hold my children close and point in the air as the fireworks light up the night. And then I'll smoke and I'll drink as my roots sink back into the ground and pull spiritual nourishment from the place where I grew up.

JULY 5, 2005

Newspaper Town

I've spent the bulk of this week in my hometown of Garden City, N.Y., in the heart of Nassau County on Long Island.

Things are different up here.

People use their car horns with much more frequency, and I've been flipped off more times this week than in the past year in Greensboro. It's comforting, in a way.

And, of course, pretty much everything costs more in New York, starting with gasoline, which is creeping steadily toward $4.50 a gallon. People complain, but the roads still snarl with traffic, and you can't find a parking spot anywhere.

The New York metropolitan area has changed since I left 20 years ago, before Rudy Giuliani made the streets safer, before the trustafarians and I-bankers made Manhattan inaccessible for regular folk, and the hipsters moved to Brooklyn.

I saw people windsurfing and kitesurfing in Brooklyn just the other day, off Coney Island within plain sight of the Belt Parkway, which in my antiquated view is kind of disturbing. These are strange times, indeed.

But they still spray graffiti on every available surface around here, still carry inexplicable affection for the New York Mets, and still consider themselves to be the world's foremost experts on pizza and bagels. A lot of them still smoke, even though cigarettes are eight bucks a pack.

And people still read newspapers. Several of them. Every day.

My father is fairly representative of New Yorkers his age. He begins each day with a run to the newsstand to get the papers. He'll pick up the *New York Times, Newsday,* the *New York Post,* and the *Daily News.* He'll get the *Village Voice* if he makes it into the city. He'll grab a *Long Island Press* every week. He avidly reads the *Garden City News* and *Garden City Life,* the two community weeklies that cover my hometown, and he still watches both the morning and evening local news, listening to 24-hour news radio in the hours in between.

When he and I talk about the future of the daily newspaper, he listens but doesn't quite believe me.

He cannot envision, for instance, a world without actual newspapers, the kind you hold in your hand, tuck into your briefcase, or take into the bathroom with you. A newspaper's website means nothing to him — he's 65 years old and he's never been on the Internet, never sent an e-mail, and only reads my articles after my mother has downloaded them through her dial-up connection and printed them out.

He's old school, to be sure.

While my parents have been getting their fill of the grandchildren, I have been spending some time in the apartment where they live, sitting in my father's chair, watching his television, and eating his snacks.

The front room is filled with newspapers, fresh ones each day that are regularly piled on a side table before a weekly dispatch to the recycling bin. There are generally several more scattered within reach of my father's chair in various stages of ingestion.

My father doesn't just read newspapers; he devours them. He reads most every local news article, though there is plenty of overlap in the New York tabloid dailies. He looks at box scores and studies league standings in the sports pages, no matter what season is running. He pulls out the TV listings and leaves them on his table, regularly consulting them throughout the day. He does the crossword puzzle, but only in the *Times.* I am pretty sure he scans the obituaries, and maybe even the classifieds. These papers not only keep him abreast of happenings in the area in which he lives, but they also help define the world around him. I don't know what my father would do without his daily newspapers. I don't know because I've never seen him without them.

I have heard from people who know about such things that daily newspapers are dinosaurs, that they must change their focus or die trying. I am acutely aware of layoffs, shrinking page sizes, shuttered bureaus, and the mantra of "more with less," things that are now a part of the culture at daily newspapers everywhere.

I have read that dailies will soon be free, and that eventually, in 35 years or so, that the print product will cease to exist. I tell my father these things when we talk about the business.

He has a newspaper in his lap when I give him this forecast, spell out for him the dismal and declining state of the industry, reinforce the notion that the eyeballs are moving online and that is eventually where everything will be, and that if he wants to continue to slake his insatiable thirst for news he better get with the program and spend a little time with my mother's dial-up connection.

He still doesn't quite believe me, or maybe he just doesn't care.

"In 35 years," he tells me, "I don't think I'm gonna have to worry about it."

JULY 1, 2008

Fire Island, the Skier, and the Ten Ant

The army ant general lined up his ten best ants and paced in front of them. He got right into the first soldier's proboscis and gave him his marching orders.

"I want you to go out there and tell the truth! Now go! Go!" And off the first ant scurried, to go tell the truth. The army ant general went on down the line, giving similar orders to all his best soldiers: "Tell the truth!" "Tell it like it is, ant!" "Be honest, you mud-crawling, exoskeletal bastard!" And so on. But then the general got to the tenth ant, and he had a different set of instructions for this last soldier.

"Lie, you ten ant," he said.

And that is how you spell "lieutenant." LIE-U-TEN-ANT.

The story comes courtesy of one of my favorite teachers, Mrs. Bohlin, who passed last week after a battle with Alzheimer's disease. I haven't seen her in years, and already I miss her terribly.

I often credit my mother, also an English teacher, with my proclivity for the written word, but it would be disingenuous not to acknowledge Mrs. Bohlin's contributions to my abilities as a reader, a writer, and a thinker.

I learned more about Ann Bohlin from her obituary than I ever learned about her in class. I did not know, for example, that she was from Chicago, because I was too young when I knew her to place her flat Midwestern accent. I didn't know she held a master's degree from the University of Wisconsin-Madison, which she likely got at a preternaturally young age. And I didn't realize she spent her entire

41-year career in the same school.

I met her on my first day of seventh-grade in 1982. They called it Garden City Junior High back then, grades seven through nine. A group of about 30 of us had been culled from the general population and installed in a program designed to enrich the young minds of those deemed scholastically talented and gifted. Everybody else called us "TAG fags," which, of course, is what we now call ourselves when we mess with each other on Facebook.

Mrs. Bohlin was the anchor of a teaching crew assigned to shepherd this group of bright, socially awkward adolescents, and she dove right in with *Bless the Beasts and Children* by Glendon Swarthout, a novel about a band of troubled misfit teenagers who sneak out of camp to free a doomed herd of bison. It resonated with me and my fellow dweebs like a gong in the bathroom.

She also had us turn out the lights and stare at candles or free write. Sometimes she would take us outside and have us sketch trees and buildings. For individual projects, we could choose any form we wanted: art, writing, music, carpentry. She helped me write my first play in the spring of '83, a murder mystery that took place in the network of trails that laced across Fire Island. No one had ever told me that 12-year-olds didn't write plays, and Mrs. Bohlin sure wasn't going to be the first. We produced and performed it right there in her classroom.

Oh, she had my number all right. She had all of our numbers. Most teachers consider themselves fortunate if they can reach one or two students a year. Mrs. Bohlin touched us all; the threads on Facebook can attest to that.

Mrs. Bohlin loved Fire Island; she and her husband, Dr. Bohlin, had a house there. Every spring they would take students to the island, a quick bus trip from Garden City. We'd run down sand dunes, take pictures of wildlife, sketch the beach grass, and eat PBJs with sand in them. I still remember my trip there, particularly the ride home, which I spent making out in the back of the bus with my nerdy but awesome girlfriend while Eddie Grant's "Electric Avenue" played on a boom box.

Are you out there, Alex?

But what I will always remember are my teacher's mnemonics. Mrs. Bohlin had a wonderful mind, and she was as strict a grammarian as ever I've encountered. She taught us prepositions by drawing a mountain on the chalkboard with a skier on it and the sentence, "The skier went [blank] the mountain." The preposition, she explained, was the word that went in the blank: down, across, through, along, under, beneath, inside … whatever. They were all prepositions. I think about that all the time.

I will also never forget how to spell "rhythm," because rats have yellow teeth. Get it? R-H-Y-T and you're pretty much home.

She had a spelling trick for the word "medieval," which escapes my somewhat damaged memory. But her masterwork, her *pièce de résistance,* was the song she sang to the tune of "Mary Had a Little Lamb" about the helping verbs.

Am is are was were be been
Have has had, do does did.
May might can could shall should will would
Are the helping verbs.
Must!

"Don't forget the 'must,'" she used to say. "That's the best part."

July 17, 2009

AFTER NINETY YEARS, A GATHERING

Lewis Pagano, DDS (retired), shifted somewhat uncomfortably in the ladder-backed chair in his youngest daughter's living room. It was his 90th birthday party, and Lewis, the last of seven children born to Italian immigrants in Morristown, N.J., must have experienced a form of *deja vu*. His older brother — Tony Pagano, 91 — made slow laps around the buffet table as each new course appeared. And his older sister, Olympia Falgione, 93, shouted questions at her daughter Aleta concerning exactly how these people at the party were related to her.

"Which one is that?"

"That's Bobbie, ma."

"Bobbie?"

"Bobbie! She's Lew's daughter!"

"And who is that one?"

"Ma!"

This is the family into which I was born in 1970. Lew is my grandfather; Aleta, my cousin. The room is filled with people who have the same nose as I do, the same crinkle about the eye and Neanderthal brow, the same receding hairline and predisposition to gout. We shout over each other and talk with our hands, swarm over the cheese plate, step down into the basement to see what the children are up to.

It's the kind of thing my family used to do all the time when I was growing up: gather together in someone's house for a birthday, a holiday, a fresh bottle of Scotch … whatever excuse was handy for assembling a big tray of baked ziti and a few loaves of fresh, crusty bread.

Only we haven't done anything like this in decades. I haven't seen my cousins Aleta and her sister, Lynette, in a good ten years. Uncle Tony, who was a vibrant, swarthy man lumbering about the Pagano junkyard in Morristown the last time I saw him — which may have been 20 years ago — is now, well … an old man. And my Aunt Olympia, who used to remind me a little bit of the Bride of Frankenstein because of the twin white streaks she maintained in her jet-black hair, is still as feisty as a 93-year-old woman can be, though these days you have to be conscious which is her "good" ear.

"Which one is that? Is that Lisa? Who are the little ones?"

"Ma!"

It's all coming back to me: the bus in the junkyard where the brothers would eat crackers and drink Scotch, Christmases at my grandfather's house in Morristown with *torrone* candy and Italian cookies, aging relatives sitting on lawn chairs at family barbecues, the weddings, the funerals, the card games, the gossip.

And always the roar of conversation, the stories that gain power in the retelling, the exclamations of made-up words in Italian.

"Disgustinad!" says my cousin Joe.

I had forgotten we could do that.

This event, unlike all those ghosted memories, is a catered affair, with rare roast beef and onion marmalade piled atop crostini, raw vegetables and dip, a wedge of horseradish cheddar, pigs in blankets. But come dessert time, our heritage asserts itself in the tray of cake-like *taralle* cookies Aleta made; my cousin Geraldine's ricotta cake, which gets swept up in about a minute and the recipe for which Geraldine will not share; a couple buckets of *sfogliatelle,* that flaky pastry that looks like a clamshell filled with ricotta custard, procured from a local Italian bakery — no one in my family makes *sfogliatelle* anymore.

Around the house stand pictures of my grandfather at various stages of his life: his graduation from dental school at the University of Pennsylvania; his marriage to my grandmother, the former Josephine DeSantis; his time in the Army toward the end of World War II; a shot of him in his 50s, at the top of his game with a cigar and a grin.

There are a hundred stories here, some of them colorful family histories that my grandmother says I can only write about after she's dead — a statement that may sound morbid to non-Italians, but rest assured that Italians make pronouncements like that all the time. There is the immigration song written when Pellegrino Pagano brought his wife, Brigida, to the new world, sired seven children, and began to prosper. There are the sad ballads of those we've lost along the way — my grandfather's brother Nujay and his twin, Carmen, who passed when I was only ten; Olympia's husband, Art, and his son Artie; the long list of cousins who did not make it to see this day.

A few hours in, Uncle Tony makes his way around the conversation pit, wiping crumbs from his jacket. He espies his younger brother, Lew, my grandfather, taking in the whole scene with his 90-year-old eyes, perhaps not as blazing as they once were but still able to appreciate this generational display.

Tony looks down at his brother. "I don't remember things so good anymore," he says.

My grandfather smiles up at his big brother.

"That's too bad," my grandfather says, and his eyes return to the family, to his party, to his blood.

It is his birthday, and we are all together again.

OCTOBER 28, 2009

LONG ISLAND POSTCARD

It wouldn't be Christmas without a trip to the family homestead on Long Island, although my parents sold the house years ago and now live in an apartment on Nassau Boulevard across the street from a bar that was once known as Paddy's Inn (and Whiskey Red's before that), where I've been drinking since I was about 14.

(Paddy, by the way, now lives in Greensboro, and I'll occasionally bump into him at a bar or a blues show or something and we'll talk about the old days and that guy named Paulie who used to hang out in the bathroom.)

And it wouldn't be Christmas if I didn't spend some time traveling the roads and byways of my largely misspent youth here on the island, letting the memories rise to the surface of my psyche and then wash over me in a soothing balm.

You want me to set the scene? I'll set the scene. I'm sitting in a Panera near the corner of Jericho Turnpike and Herricks Road during the lunch rush, surrounded by people with hard accents dressed in black. Traffic flows like a rushing river in the near-freezing rain, and the parking lot is a snarling tangle of angry SUV drivers giving each other the finger and a taste of the horn. There are stores and restaurants as far as the eye can see and naked black trees, their branches like streaks of India ink against the thickly clouded sky.

My high school is a mile down the road, and I can see Mama Theresa's, the pizza joint where my friends and I ate lunch nearly every day of our senior year. Were I to head east for five minutes I would come upon the mall where I worked during my teens. Just across the street from it once stood a restaurant where I tended bar for a couple years after college when I was trying to figure out just what the hell I wanted to do with my life.

If I wanted to, I could head over to Seventh Street in Garden City and stand on the corner and within a couple hours see 15 people I grew up with.

What is it about this place, as hard and cold as it is, that makes me feel so warm inside?

For me, Long Island is the ultimate known quantity, even though so much has changed in the 20 years that I've been gone.

Of course, much is still the same. The way people drive, for instance, is shameful, and if we drove a crappier car we'd ram into some of these maniacs just on principle.

I am of this place. I understand its rhythms and the motivations of its people — not always so noble, but certainly well defined. I know where to get a good ham, egg, and cheese and that a regular coffee will contain milk and sugar. The accent, which after a couple days here is starting to sneak back into my voice, sounds like a kind of music to me. And while in North Carolina I sometimes feel like an exotic and misunderstood animal, here on Long Island there are a million Irish guys with flat asses and big, red noses who truly believe the Giants can win the Super Bowl this year.

I mean, they're 10-5 as of this dispatch. That's pretty damn good.

My children have been luxuriating in the presence of their doting grandparents and my far-flung sisters who think it's hysterical when my little girl stamps her foot and tells me "No!"

My wife, who has been getting her New York on in a big way, is out making deals and lining up business, which around here is a form of entertainment and one of the things that people respect.

And I'm just soaking it all in, wondering if I could ever live up here again while knowing in both my heart and mind that I can't.

Tonight we'll see Dr. Lawyer and his wife, Dr. Doctor; there'll be wine and song, laughter and tears as our children tumble around on the floor just like the doctor and I did not so long ago. Tomorrow will be spent with one of the Mikes — half of my New York friends are named Mike — and his wife, Mrs. Mike, and maybe the Dicks will drive in from their new home in Harlem, the purchase of which has inspired me to call him the anti-George Jefferson.

Because he sold his deluxe apartment in the sky to live in Harlem, you see.

And on Saturday we'll get up before sunrise and hit the road, hoping to cross Staten Island before the heavy traffic sets in. We'll bring bagels, each one big as a baby's head, eat them on the road, and remember our trip. And before dinner we should be back in Carolina, except for the pieces of us we left behind.

JANUARY 2, 2008

PART 5

ARTIFACTS

Cool Guy Vest

I call it the Cool Guy Vest, and I'm wearing it today. It's made of brushed black suede, shiny satin, and sturdy steel snaps. Totally bad-ass.

I picked it up more than 15 years ago in, of all places, the Louisiana Superdome during one of those huge mega-closeout sales that hinge on the bait and switch.

I was a recent college graduate, rededicated to the idea of living in New Orleans and tending bar for a living while freelancing some journalism on the side. I had just signed a lease on a Garden District apartment, of which I would be the sole resident, my first time living alone. My primary relationship was with a woman from the West Bank, but I had big plans for my genitals in the coming months — I was kind of a bastard back then, but I reasoned that I had been waiting my entire life to be out of school and earning money and that I was beholden to no one. I envisioned the next few years as a seamless binge of wine and women and song, a celebration of a young man hitting his stride.

It worked out pretty much as I planned.

But the vest … man, the vest … I remember seeing it amongst all the junk stacked in piles in one of the Superdome's adjunct chambers. I was there for a VCR, one of those newfangled ones where you could tape programs by punching in a numerical code, and I had slipped under the leather guy's tent just because … I don't know … something about the smell … like a catcher's mitt or a saddle or a really good pair of shoes. Leather. Nothing else like it. And as a young man about to prove his mettle to the city of New Orleans, I was pretty sure I was gonna need some. Or, at least, some suede.

It cost me 12 bucks. Over the years, I've worn the Cool Guy Vest behind the bar, on New Year's Eve and Halloween. I've paired it with T-shirts and jeans, blazers and Henleys, neckties and bolos. I've worn it under a tuxedo and with practically nothing else at all.

And like I said, I'm wearing it today. Maybe it sounds pretty stupid, but this piece of clothing, which is older than my children, my marriage, my career ... hell, it's older than my house ... it makes me remember that bold and feisty young man ready to grab his life by the throat and throttle it until it coughed up its prizes; it reminds me of the bits of him that remain. The Cool Guy Vest is a part of me, and when I wear it I am gonna eat your lunch.

I know that the Cool Guy Vest is just a representation of those qualities I associate with it, qualities that exist in me whether I'm wearing the vest or not. But I still like having the vest, even though I don't wear it all that much anymore. Not often at all.

Recently a friend lost something. Several somethings, actually: more than a dozen guitars he's been collecting since he was 12 that are worth perhaps six figures at fair market value.

Their emotional value is inestimable.

The reasons behind the loss aren't important for this story. What's important is that he gathered them one by one at various noteworthy intersections of his life. He had them for a time and now he doesn't. Like the Cool Guy Vest, these guitars mattered to him for the things they stood for, their relationship to the turns in his life story. Losing them in a single instant was like losing crucial chapters of his own history — or, at least, the physical manifestations of them.

Stuff is like that — these things we own that also, in a way, own us.

My friend is choosing to be philosophical about the whole thing.

"Maybe that's what happens," he said to me. "Maybe you finally become an adult when all those things you have that tie you to the past are gone."

That's one way to look at it. If that's true, then all this stuff we have — these things we've amassed that make us feel complete, that help us define who we are — all this stuff is holding us back, keeping us from truly moving forward, away from what was and toward what could be.

The problem is that some of that stuff from the past is worth keeping.

Maybe my friend has moved on from the loss of his guitars, but I'm pretty sure he'd take them back if given the choice.

And at this point in my life, I am unwilling to give up the Cool Guy Vest. I've got it on right now, and I am ready to take on the world.

NOVEMBER 18, 2009

The Perfect Pair of Levi's

I'm a blue jeans kind of guy.

I don't mean that as a metaphor: I'm not rough and tumble; I don't like open spaces; and I don't know how to do anything with my hands. I can't build things or even fix them, unless the problem you've got is a dangling participle.

No, I'm a blue jeans guy simply because I like to wear blue jeans. I always have, even through the late '70s corduroy craze and the inexplicable infestation of pleated khaki that began around '82 and still persists in some circles today.

And while I'll admit to sampling liberally from the canon of denim choices over the years — I've worn Wranglers and Lees; carpenter jeans and fashionably stressed-out low-risers; I've even, God help me, worn acid wash — when it comes right down to it, there's nothing better than a pair of Levi's.

Not the phat-leg, not the button-fly, not the fancy-pocket or the bell-bottom or any of the low-slung, low-end imitators in the venerable line. Not the pre-washed or the stone-washed or anything made to look like it's already been worn for a year. I'm talking about regular, plain old Levis. Stiff, raw denim. With a leather label on the waistband and a little red tag on the butt.

There is no substitute.

I don't know why, but nobody has been able to duplicate the classic Levi jean. Either the denim isn't right or the cut is all wrong or the pockets are sewn in some weird place in the back.

And nothing wears down like a pair of Levi's, except for maybe a properly broken-in baseball mitt. After a hundred wears or so the color fades just right; the seams give in just so; frays at the cuffs and pockets attest to the art of imperfection.

At one time in my life, when I was tending bar four nights a week, I was so expert and expedient at breaking in new jeans that people would want me to break in their jeans for them. I couldn't do it, of course — you can no more break in a man's Levis than you can lose his virginity for him. There are some things we've got to do for ourselves.

But bartending was a great way to break in a pair of jeans: lots of motion and potential for scuffing, occasional spillage to critical areas, cultivated wear at the pockets and cuffs.

What I wouldn't give for a pair of Levi's trained to my own sweet hide right about now.

In the last six weeks or so I've been experiencing a blue jean crisis, and it looks like I won't be out of it for another six months.

When I was a young boy, my jeans always gave at the knees, usually after sandlot football games, bicycle spills, or particularly aggressive rounds of an activity we called "mush," better known as "kill the guy with the ball." But as I got older, a peculiarity of the male Clarey physique, one that can be described as "lack of buttock," put the stress in my blue jeans across the hips. As a result, I've blown out the ass in every pair of jeans I've had since high school. Usually, it happens in public.

But because each pair of jeans is its own entity, with its own aging pattern and life span, this is something that generally only happens to me a few times a year.

This was a bad year.

It started out well. You see, a pair of jeans grows more cultured and beautiful with each wash and wear, the fringes delicately unspooling until, inevitably, the center gives. But the moment before dissolution is not unlike the zenith of a sunset or the final throes of autumn: The jeans reach that state of near perfection and earned beauty that we earnestly strive for and rarely attain.

That's how I started the year: with a fine rotation of jeans, each approaching its own brand of nirvana. For a few months I styled them with boots and blazers and rough leather belts, basking in their faded glory.

And then the ass blew out.

It happened first on a trusty old pair of Levi's, perhaps the last pair I seasoned behind the bar. I put them on one cold morning straight from the dryer, as warm and comforting as a cake your momma baked, and when I bent over for a sock or something a fault line opened along one of the rear pockets.

A month or so later another pair, this time a well-worn denim that was nearly black at the time of purchase, gave out in precisely the same manner.

And just last week I tore the butt out of my final pair of old jeans when I hopped on a newspaper box outside the office.

My wife says she's never seen anything like it.

The long and short of it is that, as of press time, every pair of jeans in my collection is brand new, seams intact, stiff at the crotch and waist, the denim a uniform blue and the numbers on the leather waist tag clearly visible.

It's gonna take me forever to make 'em look right.

JULY 25, 2006

What Happens
When Your Stuff Owns You?

My trapezius muscles are killing me. Likewise my deltoids, my rhomboids, and my vastus lateralis. My sacrospinalis, on either side of my backbone down in the lumbar region, may hurt most of all, except for the spiny twinge of gout that's settling into my big toe on the right side.

The gout, a genetic gift from my maternal grandfather and my father both, is likely a manifestation of the poor lifestyle choices I cumulatively made over the past few weeks. But the muscle aches I came by honestly: This weekend I helped my in-laws with their last big move: a jump from a five-bedroom colonial in Summerfield, N.C., to a double-wide across the county line in Reidsville. It will act as a storage facility/living space while they spend the first idle years of their retirement cruising the country in a Fifth Wheel camper that is nicer inside than any apartment I've ever lived in.

This is the third such relocation I've been a part of. A few years ago I filled a truck with furniture and kitchen hardware when my grandmother went to join my grandfather in the New Jersey assisted living community where they still reside. And about ten years ago I helped my parents after they sold their house and became renters for the first time since they were newlyweds.

I'm fascinated by the accumulations of older people, the detritus of long lives well spent. My grandmother had in her basement a 50-year-old bottle of bitters with a first-aid cross on its side. My father held on to a set of mechanical drafting tools from college long after computer-animated design rendered them obsolete and long after he had abandoned architecture for the law.

My grandmother and father kept these things for some reason. And now, for some reason, I have these things in my house.

But nothing I've ever lugged compares to the trove packed away in carefully labeled boxes by my mother- and father-in-law.

Old farming tools. Jars filled with buttons. Crates of videotapes that soon will be unwatchable due to technological advances and physical decay. Six pie pans. Forty-five knives. Silver and china from three families. An old barn door. Rotting wood planks wrapped in old newspapers. Old newspapers saved in an old suitcase. Old suitcases made of tin, steel, cardboard, plastic. Two hundred doilies. A brick- and lead-lined kiln. Documents documents documents; books books books. A hand-held scythe. Canning jars. Brewing bottles. A Depression-era safe. A clipped ponytail from 1958. A milk jug. Dozens of baby books, scores of family portraits, hundreds of photo albums. A washtub. Enough antiques to make a homosexual's toes curl. And the oldest tennis racket I have ever seen: wooden, bereft of grip tape, and stored in a ... a pouch, I guess ... only there was no zipper. It folded over like an envelope. Zippers were for rich folk.

There was more. A lot more. And because I am something of an insensitive jerk, I found myself needling my father-in-law all weekend.

"When's the next time you plan to use this slide projector, Jim?" and "You think you're gonna lay hands on those canning jars in the next few years?" and "I'm not sure you're gonna fit three couches and two bookshelves into that double-wide."

My parents, from lines of Italian- and Irish-Americans fairly devoid of sentimentality, viewed their downsizing as a great purge, and the curbside was lined with garbage bags and crates three deep in the last few weeks they spent in their house.

Not so with the in-laws, who hail from hearty Kansas stock and did a bit of hopping around before settling in the Greensboro area in 1984.

Some of their stuff goes back six generations, when Samuel and Catherine Straily built the big barn across the road from the three-story family house in Hayes, Kansas, on land bought from the Union Pacific Railroad. The door is from that barn, leveled when the estate sold after Grandma Betty passed in 2001.

And heartless bastard though I may be, while carting this stuff off and trucking it over the county line, something began to take shape for me: a sense of generations past and of the power of artifacts to connect us with those who have gone before us. Here are the scissors that the Strailys used to cut the legs off chickens. There is the washtub that rinsed Ginny's and Uncle Jack's school clothes. The scythe that reaped thousands of acres of wheat and milo before outlasting its usefulness. The banged-up cabinet that was the first store-bought piece of furniture my wife's great-great-greats ever put in their house.

I started to get it.

So I eased up on my father-in-law who, I realized, is acting out of love and duty, as he sees himself as custodian and curator of the family archives. These things have been accumulating for six generations, and he and my mother-in-law are certainly not going to be the ones to drop the ball.

And then, as we unloaded meticulously labeled crates into his new garage, he dropped me a sly wink.

"You know," he said, "when we're gone, a third of this stuff becomes yours."

APRIL 8, 2008

Ghost of Christmas Past

The house seems quiet on those rare occasions when all the kids are asleep and I'm home alone, awake, uncomfortable in the stillness.

The wife is off to South Carolina to run a half-marathon for cancer research — a noble pursuit, to be sure, an amazing feat of discipline and focus. We are proud of her from afar and have spent the weekend cleaning the house in her honor. Her absence is keenly felt.

Going from a houseful of rambunctious children to this eerie quietude is a jarring transition, one that invites reminiscences and philosophical thought, particularly during this most nostalgic time of year.

The tree stands in the corner by the back door, ready to receive its blessing of lights and ornamentation. The decorations, descended from the attic, are stacked in boxes by the hallway and await affixture to mantles and window sashes and doorways. There will be lights and candy canes. There will be stockings and Santa hats. There will be happiness and cheer.

Yes, it's Christmastime, and even I am not immune to the stirrings of goodwill and generosity that fill the air as sure as the scent of pine needles and chestnut farts. Even I take pleasure in roaring fires, whiskey-laced eggnog, and the wanton spending spree that passes for holiday spirit these days. Even I recast barely remembered Christmases past in warm Technicolor tones.

Way back when, so long ago that I can't even pinpoint the date, I had a Christmas surprise. Under my section of the tree on Christmas morning — tucked among sweaters I didn't want, slacks that would itch my thighs, superhero Colorforms (whatever happened to Colorforms?), and a snappy new box of crayons — sat a genuine toy.

A real toy, made of wood and metal, carefully crafted and painted, designed to last the ages.

It was a fort, which back in 1976 or so was a holdover from the days when children played with such things.

Toy soldiers, of course, are designed to indoctrinate our children into militaristic ways, to prepare them for service to their country, for battle. I didn't know any of this then, of course. I just knew Santa had brought me this cool fort with cavalrymen on horseback, riflemen on foot, and howling braves wielding tomahawks. I didn't even know I wanted that fort, but it was awesome … for awhile, anyway. Like every other toy I ever had, it soon lost its luster and receded from my childhood storyline. But I remember the morning as perhaps the last bit of Christmas magic in which I truly believed.

My children still believe in Santa Claus — at least they say they do. The boys are old enough that believing in the fat man in the red suit cramps their emerging styles — both say they are the only ones in their classes who still carry the faith. That's what they say, anyway.

———————

I suppose I'll have to tell them soon, tell them how their mother and I try to scrape a Christmas together each year; how we fret and worry and plan; how we've been filling their heads with these sugarplum visions; and then, once we get them to sleep, make Christmas magic in between sips of dark beer and dew-eyed recollections.

Telling them the real story will be the end of something, for sure.

It will be a lean Christmas this year, for us and for nearly everyone we know whose fortunes are tied to the ebb and flow of labor and commerce. It will be helpful for the kids to know that the lack of abundance under the tree does not directly correlate to their be-havior this year — does not, in fact, correlate to anything other than time and money, both of which have been in short supply lately for their mother and me.

We will fill the void with stories about friends of ours who haven't had regular paychecks since before the Fourth of July, who have lost loved ones this year, or gotten the kind of terrible news that changes lives forever. We will fill it with love, and we will try to impart some sense of the greater meaning of this holiday without bribing them with an exuberance of gifts.

But I still have a trick up my sleeve. On Christmas night we'll all be staying at my uncle's house in New Jersey. There, up in the attic, he has kept all these years my wooden fort with the tiny toy soldiers and Indians. After the family has all gone home and the Christmas cookies have been polished off, we plan to set that fort up, my uncle and I, and see if it still holds enough Christmas magic to charm my two young boys.

DECEMBER 16, 2009

The Home of the Free

When Black Friday comes, the stores hire extra help. They've got attendants waving traffic in the parking lots, extra shopping bags and gift boxes stacked below the counters, plenty of small bills and coins in the registers.

When Black Friday comes, the seasoned shoppers lay out game plans and itineraries, create budgets to blow, and sharpen their elbows while amateurs get trapped in auxiliary parking lots and interminably slow checkout lines.

But when Black Friday comes to Greensboro's Glenwood neighborhood, it does so with more of a smile than a grimace, more of a conscious awareness of this compulsion to consume that seems to grip us all as the days grow short.

"The big idea is to get people to stop and think how much they're consuming," says Kathy Clark, squinting behind her sunglasses against the early afternoon glare. She's been organizing the Really, Really Free Market here at the Hive, Glenwood's non-profit community collective, for two years.

"It's in conjunction with AdBuster's Buy Nothing campaign," she says. "Instead of consuming more, buy nothing."

So while bank balances deplete across the nation, here, at the market held in the Hive's parking lot, true giving remains.

There's something vaguely un-American, if not downright unpatriotic, about getting something for nothing, as people are doing all around me right now. It's a subversive concept in an era in which we have been conditioned to believe that our spending habits fuel our economy. But the Really, Really Free Market comes at a good time, with unemployment figures topping ten percent and many families apprehensive about what the coming year will bring.

There are warm clothes here: sweaters, sweatpants, jackets, and hats awaiting the chance to once again fight off January chills. There are cases of CDs by artists you've never heard of, unless you're a fan of the band Romance's work on *The Divide* or had been hoping to stumble across a copy of Alice Gomez's *The Healing Flute.*

Other treasures lurk amongst the piles: shoes, ladies' office attire, model railroad magazines from the 1970s, a good-as-new scanner and computer keyboard, lampshades, video cables, and a roll of pink bubble wrap.

Along the side of the building runs a table loaded with produce: peppers, cukes, a bucket of kale, and some questionable mangoes. There are books: schoolbooks and self-help books and picture books and paperback novels. There are pictures without frames, frames without pictures, and look, right over there, a perfectly good Panama hat.

Nick Fields holds up an extra-large, candy-striped nightshirt, and compares it to his slight frame.

"I'm probably going to take it," he says. "I am going to make it into a fire-eating tunic."

Over at his table, a couple of women in jeans and suede boots pull a long woolen stocking from the pile.

"That is a vintage 1970s toe sock," Fields says, "from my grandmother's closet."

"I'm gonna wear these," one of the women says, pulling off her boots right then and there.

The "shoppers" are a mix of young and old, politically motivated and flat broke. There are hipsters and homeless, neighborhood folk and out-of-towners, takers and givers ... most of us fall somewhere in the middle.

I score a copy of an April 1975 issue of *Argosy: Man's World of*

Adventure magazine, which contains survival stories, war tales, fishing yarns, a piece on Bigfoot, and a cover story about the human cannonball from the circus. Bearded models in suede leisure suits, brazenly bearing chest hair, testify frankly about their cigarette preferences and a fondness for an exercise device known as the "Bullworker."

The magazine is awesome. I also grab a British joke book for the kids. Sample: "What is a sea monster's favourite fast food? Fish and ships!" I think it's gonna kill. Two kids squat by a box of toys on the parking-lot pavement. They have no idea who the California Raisins are, but they like the figurine they find of one and make him prance along the precipice of the cardboard box where he had been living, probably since the days when he was big-time.

The shadows of the children grow long on the ground. And still people come, bearing boxes and baskets, armloads of gear: a wine rack, a dartboard, a pair of rollerblades size 11, a brand-new garment bag fresh out of the box. New inventory is eagerly sorted and evaluated.

"Every year I struggle to find meaning in the season," Clark says. "It's been increasingly difficult. Is the spirit of giving compelling us to go out and buy a bunch of stuff?"

As she surveys the free market, a man from the neighborhood heads back home, a grocery bag of yellowing kale and patchy limes tucked under his arm. He is beaming.

"People who have stuff drop it off, people who need stuff come and get it," Clark says. "It makes more sense this way."

DECEMBER 2, 2009

PART 6

THE BACK NINE

The Affliction of Kings

I'm in agony.

My left foot is swollen like a fat man's fist, the big toe full as a sausage and the ball underneath throbbing like an alien pulse. When I stand and the blood rushes to my appendage, it reawakens raw nerve endings and brings the kind of pain that makes my hands shake. When I try to walk, each step conveys a thousand needles that jab into the ligatures connecting my toe to its foot. I have considered home amputation of this toe — how I would do it, where I would make the first cut — before passing out in fevered pain.

It's been like this for five days now, and it's my own damn fault.

Like Ben Franklin, Thomas Jefferson, King Henry VIII, and my father, I suffer from occasional flare-ups of the gout. The pain is so incredible that when talking about this malady I give it the respect of a definite article: I call it "the gout."

I've broken bones, endured concussions and cuttings, been bitten by spiders and stung by bees. I've torn off toenails, had my fingers smashed in doors, had my mouth and nose bashed in a time or two. Years ago, I took a tumble down a hill on the Georgetown University campus that scraped all the skin from one side of my face. The gout makes pikers of all these insults and injuries. It is the purest form of pain I've endured.

They call the gout the "rich man's disease," the "affliction of kings," because its onset is preceded by overzealous ingestion of red meat, alcohol, shellfish, sugar — all that good stuff.

To understand the disease, one must look back to rudimentary biology: the pH scale and the principles of acidity and alkalinity. Rich foods are generally acidic in nature, and their consumption lowers the pH of the consuming body. When the bloodstream becomes overly acidic, it cannot fully dissolve uric acid, an organic waste compound of carbon, nitrogen, oxygen, and hydrogen ($C_5H_4N_4O_3$). Undissolved uric acid then collects in the form of crystals in the bottom joint of the big toe. The effect is threefold: The sharp crystals more or less shred the cartilage and tendons in the toe joint; then the area swells and becomes sensitive to touch, pressure, even a good breeze; finally, in prolonged afflictions, the muscles in the area begin to cramp and seize, and you can't massage them because that aggravates the condition.

I first became afflicted with this form of arthritis about ten years ago, when most of my work was done on my feet, and I blamed the pain and swelling on hard labor and improper footwear. My wife, a naturopath, identified it as gout about five years ago and showed me how easily controlled it is by reducing my intake of booze, cigarettes, red meat, processed foods, and other things I love.

I am not a chronic sufferer — I have had three bouts in the last five years, — and the one against which I now clench my jaw is not even the worst.

I'll tell you about that attack: It was four years ago, when I was doing a lot of travel writing, and the pain grew worse over four days. I brought the gout with me on assignment to Harkers Island, N.C., for a boating story. I spent the day crunching ibuprofen and leaning on my cane.

Yes, my cane.

From Wikipedia: "Gout was traditionally viewed as a disease of the decadent and indolent, because the foods which contribute to its development were only available in quantity to the wealthy. The stereotypical victim was a lazy, obese middle-aged man who habitually overindulged in rich foods and alcohol, with port wine consumption often cited as a specific cause. This stereotype is especially evident when gout is referred to as 'The Disease of Kings.'"

Kings, my ass.

These days, I'd argue, the gout is more prevalent among those who eat cheeseburgers and drink domestic beer, available in quantity to just about everybody. In the United States gout is twice as common in African-American males as Caucasians, and occurs with some frequency in New Zealanders and Pacific Islanders. Maybe because they eat so much Spam?

I hardly consider myself a prime candidate. I exercise. I eat raw food. I eat red meat maybe three times a week, and I weigh less than I did after my freshman year of college.

But then …

My affinity for beer is well known, as is my love of cigarettes and roast beef. Also, at 37, I could technically be considered middle-aged, as horrifying as it is to think of myself as such. And for most of my life I didn't take very good care of myself because, let's face it, I didn't think I was going to live this long.

No matter.

For now, I'm drinking cherry juice and staying off the booze. I'm keeping still enough so that the uric acid crystals in my toe don't do further damage to the joint. I have a list of alkaline foods and I'm eating them — last night I had a raw organic beet for dinner.

And from now on, I'm gonna respect the gout.

July 31, 2007

Modeling Language for Children

Other working families, especially those with young children, can sympathize with the pace and tenor of our household — mornings are a loosely choreographed blur of breakfast-making, backpack-loading, and potty-sitting; evenings are a prolonged recon mission that takes us to the far corners of the city and involves much fastening of seatbelts and eating of snackage. Evening meals, when fortune grants them, are chaotic episodes of small crowd control that can sometimes result in a test of wills involving uneaten noodles. Dirty clothes and sauce-encrusted dishes pile up hourly. Cherished household items are routinely destroyed or rendered useless. Things disappear when you set them down for 30 seconds.

The lifestyle can be frustrating, especially for a man like me.

I'm a bit of a control freak, prone to arm-waving, profanity-laden outbursts when things don't go as I think they should. This is something that happens once a week in my house, usually when someone carelessly trips over my laptop's recharging cord or beats up on his little brother.

Stop hitting your brother!

Like that, except with more ... colorful language.

I remember when I first heard the vast trove of dirty words — my father unleashed the whole canon one evening after he barked his shins against an open dishwasher door. I was just five years old, but even I knew the sounds coming from his mouth, delivered with such vehemence and fury, had power.

I wasn't scared. Not really. I was, however, fascinated.

My own early experiments with the low speech were character-ized by misfires and poor syntax, but I quickly learned the grammar. The F-word is not an adjective unless you add the prefix "ing" and is tricky to convert into an adverb; the S-word, a handy one indeed, can be deployed with inflections giving it a wide array of meanings. And by the time I was 13 I could string together some colorful sentences. Working in bars for 15 years was like going to finishing school; the only place where people speak more coarsely is in restaurant kitch-ens, and I could always hold my own in them, too.

The problem, of course, is that I have children, three very ob-servant children who are in a phase of their development the head-shrinkers call "modeling." That means they watch me and then do like I do.

Greater intellects and mouths more foul than mine have grap-pled with the dilemma of preventing their children from speaking like Bourbon Street whores. But I'm a man who toils in words every day. I understand their power, yet I know that words are nothing to be afraid of. And, I reasoned back before my kids started speaking in full sentences, if they know the meaning behind the words, perhaps it will take some of their mysteries away.

Ten years ago, even five years ago, I would have laughed riot-ously at cursing children. It's funny in a Jimmy Kimmel kind of way, like Tanner from *The Bad News Bears*.

Then I heard my four-year-old apply the F-word as a descriptive noun to a particularly vexing wood puzzle. Nothing funny about that. Then I got this one the other day in the car:

"Daddy?" the six-year-old asked. "What's shit?"

"Uh," I said. "It's doodies."

He was surprised by this.

"It is?"

"Yeah," I said. "'Shit' is doodies. 'Ass' is a butt. 'Crap' is doodies, too."

"'Ass' is a butt?"

"Yeah."

"'Crap' is a bad word." This came from the four-year-old in the back seat.

"I don't think 'crap' is a bad word," I said through the rear-view mirror. "But you probably shouldn't say it in school."

"Oh. But Daddy, what about 'fart'?"

He's been thinking a lot about farts lately, ever since he took down the bulk of a giant can of baked beans with bacon.

"'Fart?'" I said. "I don't think so. 'Fart' was a bad word when I was a little boy, but I think the ruling has changed."

"Oh. 'Boogers' is a bad word."

He sounded uncertain.

"'Boogers' is not a bad word," I said, "but don't wipe them on the seat."

"OK," he said. "I know what to do with boogers. You rub them in your hands and they just disappear."

"Oh," I said.

"They just disappear, Daddy."

"Good boy," I said, because I didn't know what else to say.

The six-year-old rejoined the conversation.

"So 'crap' and 'farts' is not bad words."

"Yeah," I said, "but don't say them in school."

"But 'crap' just means doodies."

"I know, but people think it's rude."

"What about 'ass'?"

I had to think about that one. Because sometimes it's the only word that will do.

"Why don't you just use 'butt' instead," I said.

I could tell by the look on his face that this matter is far from over.

MARCH 6, 2007

HOME ALONE
WITH THE BACKBONE OF SOCIETY

It's 7:30 a.m., cold, and the house is quiet again after the hard burst of activity that happens here every weekday morning. The ripping staccato of alarm clocks. The donning of school uniforms. Some criticism of breakfast, no matter what it is, accompanied by threats not to eat it. An assessment of the weather and assignation of appropriate jacketry.

The boys hop to the bus stop on the corner. My wife and I still cannot bring ourselves to let them wait for their ride unwatched.

We'll usually allow ourselves a moment to be together with our coffee, with Baby Girl propped on pillows as "Noggin" imprints on her brain. Then a round of showers and wardrobe, a run to daycare, and a mad dash to our offices.

But today, I'm alone. My wife has been out of town all week, leaving the job of operations manager in this little nonprofit solely to me.

I've been making lunches, supervising homework, doing some light chauffeuring. I've been reading stories, keeping peace, soothing tears, enforcing punishments. I've been washing dishes — good lord, the dishes — and kicking the dirty clothes into roughly the same corner of the house. I've been getting my ass consistently and relentlessly beaten on a combat video game by a seven-year-old.

And honestly, if it were more than a couple days, I don't know how I would do it. I had to take a day off work just to manage this four-day stretch, and I still haven't taken out the garbage, tackled that pile of laundry in the corner, paid a bill, shopped for groceries, made a bed, or cleaned the cat box. I'm not even sure if I've fed the cats. And these kids need baths.

I also haven't gone to the gym, shaved, eaten a meal on a plate, or worn a wrinkle-free shirt. Or, you know, written my column.

She'll be back in seven hours. We miss her.

I don't want to turn this into a comedy of errors that reinforces the negative stereotype of paternal ineptitude, but the days have not been without their share of humor. Baby Girl got her foot stuck in a Lego bucket, and I found out what happens when a child vomits in a public pool. (They make everybody get out.)

This is a story about the hard labor of raising a family, the delicate balance struck between work and play and home and self, the constant physical and emotional maintenance, the times of stress and exasperation that come in between those moments that make it all worthwhile.

My wife has gotten our little nonprofit running smoothly. My usual role is unglamorous. I have some titular authority, but my duties are mostly relegated to odd afternoon pick-ups, heavy cooking, and a rotating Saturday itinerary. It's tough enough for the two of us to tackle; if I had to do everything myself for an extended period of time, I'd surely go mad.

My own mother stayed home with my sisters and me until I was in the seventh grade, when she went back to teaching school. This was in the '70s, and in my neighborhood just about everybody's mother kept the house and family while their fathers took the early train into the city and a late one back.

Back then, we took a school bus home for lunch every day, where we ate home-cooked meals in our own kitchens, and then went back for the afternoon session. Schools don't do that anymore. It's a huge waste of money, for one, but also there is nobody for kids to come home to at midday. Single and divorced parents, dual incomes, active lifestyles have left our homes empty Mondays through Fridays when the sun hangs high.

It's a whole new world out there for the American family, which has seen some major changes in the 30 years or so since my mother used to make me grilled cheeses for lunch on Wednesday afternoons.

But families — mothers, fathers, children, homes — remain as the backbone of the society we've created. We hold jobs and buy shelters to set up our little nonprofits. We use the schools and public playgrounds, log thousands of miles on the roads shuttling our little tax deductions around town, regularly redistribute our funds, and continually reinvest in our companies. And we're making a product: the next generation of entrepreneurs who will, it's hoped, one day open up little nonprofits of their own.

Right now Baby Girl is marching around the house in Dora the Explorer pajamas and green rubber boots that look like frogs. She's singing little songs to herself and peering at me from behind doorways, around corners, lugging around a small stuffed dog she calls "Kevin."

She approaches me.

"I smell like candy," she says.

This column is done.

MARCH 4, 2008

END TO PROCREATION

I'm writing this column in the throes of a perfectly legal, doctor-pre-scribed hydrocodone bender, so it's possible I may reveal more about myself than I would under more sober conditions. But what the hell ... I'm grooving like an Earth, Wind and Fire backup singer right now; and if past experience has taught me anything, it's never to fight a good buzz, especially one obtained under doctor's orders.

Hydrocodone, as the surgeon kept reminding me, is a narcotic analgesic, with side effects like lightheadedness and euphoria. It's the painkiller of choice for discriminating inebriates everywhere, including luminaries like smarmy "Friends" actor Matthew Perry and tough-guy quarterback Brett Favre, who reportedly used to pick them out of his vomit and send them on another trip down the pike.

I'm supposed to take no less than six a day. Doctor's orders.

I could go on in this vein for awhile, but I suppose I should just get to the point: I got the pills because I'm recovering from surgery. Last week I had a vasectomy. That means that in about six weeks, barring any unforeseen complications, I will be completely and more or less irreversibly sterile.

I was an excellent candidate for the procedure. My wife and I are both 35, and since spring 2000 we have had three children. Bang bang bang, just like that. Two of them are sons, so we're pretty sure the family name will continue. And there's just no way — no way — that we can possibly handle any more kids. No way.

Still, it was not an easy decision.

For starters, it is a procedure that no one in my family has considered. I may be a secular humanist, but I wasn't raised that way. The people in my family are fairly strict Catholics, and their man Pope is not cool with the concept of sex as anything other than a means of procreation.

And there's another thing: I don't like knives, needles, or any of the other sharp, pokey things they use for operations like this. I don't like doctors, nor can I stomach large amounts of blood, particularly my own. The sight of it causes a marked drop in my blood pressure, accompanied by cold sweats and a dizziness that is nowhere near as pleasurable as, say, a prolonged hydrocodone binge.

But my family's values and my own wussiness are nothing when compared to the panic I would feel were my wife to get pregnant again. I don't see how we could do it. We can't fit another child seat in our car; we have no more bedrooms in our house; and these kids we have, though we love them to the limits of our souls, are drinking the life force right out of us.

My poor wife has been either pregnant or breastfeeding since 1999, and if she doesn't get a good night's sleep soon, I fear she might take the issue of my sterilization into her own hands.

And I don't want to become one of those stereotypical Irish mooks with more kids than house, more house than money, and not enough time to tend any of it properly.

So we went ahead and booked it. For those considering the procedure, let me tell you what to expect.

Before the operation, expect to have the longest conversation about your testicles you've ever had. Expect to be examined and shaved. You also can go ahead and anticipate no small degree of awkwardness and humiliation.

Expect to be awake and coherent during the process. You can expect some initial pain as the anesthesia is administered. Then be ready for some horrible snipping sounds as your vasa deferentia, the superhighway for your genetic information, are cut and tied off. Expect to make polite conversation so you don't have to listen to the cutting. And if you peek down at what the doctor and nurse are doing, expect to be horrified.

The recovery is no big deal. The first day I felt like I had taken a serious kick to the groin by Mia Hamm wearing steel-toed boots. You're not going to want to go horseback riding, but the pain is endurable. And if you've got an appreciative wife like mine, you just might get a couple days of couch time on easy street.

The pain, which lives deep and throbbing in your pelvic region, lessens each day. The hydrocodone helps.

Another thing that lasts a few days is a vague sense of disbelief: I can't believe I just did that.

I still can't believe it — that I voluntarily gave up a piece of my manhood, that I am for all practical purposes sterile, that my doctor gave me all these pills and that I can have six of them a day.

And it's hard to believe that I'm free: free to raise my kids and to pursue my career, free for my wife and I to get on with our lives knowing that our days of diapers and baby spit are coming to an end.

Now I think it's time for my pill. ...

JANUARY 31, 2006

Blowing This Taco Stand

I've run away from home. Why? None of your damn business, that's why. Suffice it to say that, like Bill Murray's character in the film *What About Bob?*, I'm taking a vacation from my problems. I'm baby-stepping. I'm doing the work. And let me tell you, my friend, my problems are as big and nasty as a shaved-down yeti. I'm thinking it will take two days. Maybe three. It's gonna take at least eight cigars, six hours of sad songs, more or less, and approximately a gallon of Scotch.

I'm at the bar, naturally, because that's where a man like me goes when he wants to forget — at least, that's what I used to do. For the last ten years or so I've been actively trying to accumulate memories: children, milestones, accomplishments, those sweet, sweet moments that live indelibly in my memory. I haven't wanted to forget like this in awhile.

Probably never. And right now, if I could, I'd wipe at least three months away like a sneeze on a mirror. But memory doesn't work like that, and so I've made myself scarce.

I ran away from home once before. It was in 1977, back when I was a kid on Long Island. I remember it well. A Sunday it was, shortly after a disastrous session at St. Joe's church on Franklin Avenue. I didn't like church then. I don't like church now. But on that particular Sunday I was behaving worse than usual, sending my father into the kind of red rage that only an overwrought, hung-over father can muster. On this particular Sunday, he wasn't having any of it. And neither was I. I remember I was serving out a sentence in my room, pacing like I always have when in a state of high agitation. I heard them all downstairs, my parents and sisters. Laughing. Eating. Watching television. Carrying on like there wasn't a prisoner upstairs wearing a tread in the green shag carpet.

Screw it, I thought. I'm outta here. I wrote a simple note on a dry-erase board that hung on my bedroom wall, one with a picture of the cartoon character Ziggy on it, shrugging his shoulders like a chump, bitching about Mondays or some such thing.

"I can no longer live under such tyranny and mistrust," I scrawled on the board, which was pretty astute for a six-year-old. Then I crept down the stairs and slipped out the door. It occurs to me now, here at the bar, that in my current situation perhaps I am the tyrant. I am the one harboring mistrust. I know this: I have my reasons. And, as is often the case, genetics equals destiny.

It was cold — March in New York — and icy patches of melting snow obscured greening lawns in an oddly bovine pattern. I walked the curved streets of my neighborhood, registered laps on pork-chop-shaped blocks with my hands stuffed in my pockets, chuffing out steamy breaths and trying to keep warm. In my haste to escape I had forgotten to bring a jacket, and when I could no longer feel my fingers I made for the only place I knew to go: my friend Steve's house. His mother let me in; we sat at his kitchen table and had homemade snacks — his mother was a compulsive baker and also my mother's best friend. Within ten minutes of my arrival, the jig was up.

This time I have a better plan. Gone is where I'll stay — for a couple days at least — or so I'm thinking. Oblivion is what I'll embrace — not the sloppy, booze-soaked kind but the cathartic, leavening kind where floating in the ether is a choice and not a function of inebriation. Escape is what I'll seek, just like I did on that cold March day in 1977. That will show them. Or will it?

Back in 1977, I had been gone from my parents' home for what I thought was hours. But when they came to pick me up they explained to me it had just been about 45 minutes. And they were laughing! Laughing at my sense of drama, my childish outrage, my ridiculous vocabulary. Even today, when the story is retold at Christmas or Thanksgiving, it is narrated as a comedy and not a tragedy.

I thought my gesture of indignant protest would bring my parents to their knees and change the course of my family forever. It did not. And I guess it's possible that my current exodus will be misread as well, viewed not as the last meaningful act of a discontented and wronged man but as an innocuous reaction to an ugly truth that will remain the truth no matter how much Scotch gets poured.

Either way, it feels good to be gone.

AUGUST 12, 2009

A Crazy Drywall Fantasy

Had a chance to sit down with Dr. Lawyer a few weeks ago in one of our semi-regular powwows, where we kick back and really get a good look, acknowledge the last decade of our lives, and honestly assess the paths we've chosen.

I get the better end of the deal: Dr. Lawyer is a psychiatrist and also a lawyer. People pay well for his advice that I get for free because once, a long time ago, he threw up on my phone.

Like all of us, he's much more than the sum of his professions: a husband, a father, a son, a brother, a friend. And all of these roles sometimes weigh perceptibly on my pal's head. I can see it in his eyes, in the creases in his earlobes, his posture.

And there's not much I can give this guy in the way of counsel. I'm a journalist and editor, after all, and I can help him if he wants to know the name of Cleveland's biggest newspaper or if he's using too many prepositional phrases, but to ease someone's suffering is something I haven't done with any competency since I left bartending so many years ago. These days, I usually end up making people feel worse. The best I could do for Dr. Lawyer this last time was to pull out a joke that I've made ... oh... maybe a thousand times before.

"You probably should have gone to refrigeration school," I said.

He considered this carefully, as he considers just about everything.

"No," he said. "That could mean I'd have to own my own business. What I'd like, I think, is a job loading and unloading drywall for some guy."

This is funny, because the most physical job Dr. Lawyer ever held was a summer stint as a short-order cook in the cafeteria of the hospital where he now does rounds. But I didn't laugh, and neither did he. We both kind of just … fantasized about it for a moment.

Loading drywall. And then unloading it. All day, with a nice break for a homemade lunch and, very likely, a good bit of truck time in between, where we'd just ride around with the drywall on the way to the site, listening to the radio, and drinking from giant mugs of gas-station soda.

Drywall is heavy, of course, an obviously aggravating circumstance. But I'm sure you get to use a hand-truck or some such device. In fact, I once saw a lone laborer move a copy machine as big as a fat man's coffin from a second-floor office down to his van. He had a mechanized machine that secured the copier, and it climbed stairs all by itself. Surely there have been similar innovations in the drywall game.

We'd load and unload in a perfect cycle all year long, with two solid weeks of vacation, benefits, and, I don't know, maybe a discount on drywall or something. And every day about 45 minutes before quitting time, we'd load up the truck and head for home, our wives and children, and we wouldn't think about drywall again until the alarm sounded the next morning.

Hmmm …

And this working for "some guy" element … that's a fine wrinkle. It implies that we are not in management, which would preclude us from serious decision-making as it pertained to the drywall. Presumably, our boss would know something about the business, so there would be plenty of drywall to haul. And he'd probably be the mustachioed, cigar-chomping sort, brusque yet lovable, with a taste for doughnuts and frozen pot-pies.

"Your job is to load the fuckin' drywall," he'd say to us. "And then unload it. Understand, professor?"

"Professor"… what a cutup.

But here our little fantasy comes to an end. There are way too many obstacles between us and our dream jobs: student-loan debt and a philanthropic bent in his case, a bad back in mine. We have mortgages based on our current earnings — no way could we sell our houses in this real-estate market — and over the years we both have become accustomed to equating our jobs with our identities to some degree, and I'm not sure if our egos could take it.

Also, our prospects for this type of work are not good. Although we are both familiar with drywall and are fairly certain we could identify it from a group of other home-building materials, we have little experience in the industry and surely there would be others better qualified to land such great jobs. Frankly, we wouldn't even know where to begin.

Loading drywall. And then unloading it.

What were we thinking? Such a crazy dream ...

OCTOBER 22, 2008

It Wouldn't Be Father's Day Without the Kids

I'm writing this on Father's Day, with late-afternoon sun cutting through the window lace and, on the television set behind me, SpongeBob bemoaning the destruction of his pineapple under the sea.

I once had to write in silence. The delicacy of my personal genius required ... demanded ... no less. Or so I thought.

Now, that absorbent and yellow and porous fellow gives way to baths. And pizza. And popsicles. And more baths. The house is abuzz, and I'll peck out my little piece in fits and spurts as befits a man for whom delicate genius is a luxury that a house full of children simply does not afford.

We've been fishing with nightcrawlers off the pier at Lake Brandt. It was interesting to see the kids' reaction to the squiggly-squirmies. My first-born son will only touch them with a towel over his fingers, and under no circumstances will he deign to pierce one with a fish-hook. His younger brother lacks the motor skills to properly wend the worms around the barb — to my mind, anyway — but he's fascinated by the filthy little creatures nonetheless, and he prefers propping his pole on the dock and watching the bait knot up around the hook to casting it out on the water.

Baby Girl, who sometimes cries when she even thinks she sees a spider, goes wrist-deep into the bait bucket and traps worms between her chubby, mud-caked fingers. She dangles them in the air for my inspection, and then, I don't know, kind of plays with them there on the dock.

"They don't have any sleeves!" she says.

We don't make a huge deal out of Father's Day in my house. I sleep in a bit; my wife makes coffee; and I get to watch whatever I want on television. Sometimes we do brunch. Sometimes we go to a movie. Sometimes we go fishing, like we did today.

We've never caught a fish in two years of trying, which is just as well. We wouldn't know what to do with one if we did. But it's nice to sip Gatorade and watch the water and fling casts out as far as we can. Fishing, like writing, is an entirely different matter when there are young children involved.

In fact, they touch just about everything in my life. Because of my children I have different attitudes than I once did about work, family, teeth-brushing, patience, silence, television violence, and the importance of doing homework.

I also mean that literally: They touch everything. They've loosened the screws on my lawnmower, gotten nosebleeds on my pillow, and, recently, made my last pair of disposable contact lenses disappear.

I'll tell you this: They're lucky they're so damn cute and that they give me so much free fodder for my weekly column, or I swear I would have sold them off for gas money after that last act.

I exaggerate. A bit.

But truly, I do owe this lackadaisical Sunday to their existence. A man cannot be a father without children. And I owe them more than that. The best things in my life have happened since they came along, which is ironic. Upon news of my impending fatherhood all those years ago, I thought my life was over. This notion was followed by a panic attack that has yet to abate.

My kids have changed my concept of relaxation as well.

Take today. What's more relaxing than a little pier fishing on a hot Sunday afternoon, you ask? We've got three kids, none of them strong swimmers, out there on water's edge. There are openings in the deck slats to crawl through, nightcrawlers to eat, and hooks flying everywhere.

It's about as relaxing as crystal meth.

And yet ... and yet.

The things fatherhood has given me far outweigh those it has taken. No matter how many items in my house my kids destroy, no matter how many impositions they make on my time, my money, my marriage, my career, my sanity ... I'm still getting a sweetheart deal, emphasis on the "sweetheart."

It's quiet in my house now, except for an occasional stray cough from Baby Girl's bedroom in back. She's balled up under a pink blanket with princesses on it — despite my feelings on the matter I fear I will never expunge the princesses from my house — and her mother is rubbing her feet. The Brothers Clarey kneel on their bedroom carpet, a wall made of Legos between them and a deployment of Yu-Gi-Oh! cards. One last battle will rage before lights-out.

When I know they're asleep, and not a minute before, I'll sink a little deeper into the couch and try to keep my eyes open long enough to relax for an hour.

JUNE 27, 2008

Mourning for Robert

What do you do when someone you love dies? That's the question we've all been answering since my brother-in-law met his fate on a waterfront highway more than a week ago. We've found that the first thing to do is to get our heads around the situation.

It's hard to accept that someone so vibrant, someone who burned so brightly, no longer walks among us. It's hard to accept that this person who stood so reliably by us is not there anymore. Something like that takes a few days. At least. And so we walked around in a collective stupor, consoled ourselves with what few happy thoughts we could conjure, pooled our grief to make it more bearable.

Still there were details to attend to. His apartment, full of his things, each saturated with his memory, his scent. His family, which included a cadre of ex-wives, girlfriends, daughters, stepdaughters, and grandchildren, would need closure. And then there was the matter of his short but eventful life, which would need to be honored in an appropriate fashion.

As we tied up the loose ends of his existence, I became concerned with what Robert would have wanted. He would have wanted us to be together. He would have wanted us to remember him. He would have wanted a tribute.

That's why, on Thursday morning, I set out alone for Elizabeth City, N.C., where Robert's cremains awaited. It would take a week or so to get them through the mail, we were told. It didn't take 30 seconds for me to make my move. The least I can do, I thought, is to bring my boy home. It was an impulse decision, one of which I think

Robert would have approved.

Still, though … strange.

Strange to sign a piece of paper and be handed your friend's last worldly remains in a small shopping bag. Strange how heavy it was. Strange to sit on the banks of the Pasquotank River, storm surge sending tannic water lapping over the seawall and a light rain falling, while hugging a box and crying. Strange to drive 250 miles with Robert's cremated body strapped into the shotgun seat, headed west about an hour ahead of the flooding, and talking to him in a soothing voice.

Strange how much better it made me feel.

Strange, too, is what we did with him when he got to Greensboro — at least some people seemed to think it was strange. On Friday we held the Robert Striano Memorial Bar Crawl, packing him into a backpack and taking him on a tour of some of his favorite watering holes. The circuit went from Old Town to Nate's Place to Spring Garden Pizza, over to the corner of Walker and Elam for drop-ins at Walker's and Wahoo's, and then a final blitz through the Westerwood Tavern, his favorite. Perhaps two dozen of his closest friends took part in this tribute, which was well received in all the places we went. Robert would have loved it.

My wife and I, though we're not sure why, agreed that the event made us feel better about losing so suddenly someone we loved.

Then came Monday, when 200 or so of us gathered in Alumni House at the University of North Carolina at Greensboro for a proper memorial.

You can tell a lot about a person by who — if anyone — bothers to show at his funeral. Robert's tribute included dozens of family members, some of whom flew in from across the country. His brother Ron, in from Portland, Ore., looks so much like him that he got double-takes all afternoon. There were friends from the bar; former and current roommates; colleagues from every job he ever held, including staffers from UNCG, where he had worked for the last few years. When the time came for speechifying, the chairs had run out and mourners were four deep at the back of the room.

Photos of his life flickered on a big screen. His favorite songs seeped through small speakers. Tears. Laughter. Coors Light. All of that.

When a loved one dies, we are saddened, of course. We mourn for the departed, and for all those left behind in his absence. We mourn for what was and could have been, and we mourn for ourselves, as we are each ultimately destined for the same fate.

But in death there is also a celebration of a life lived.

It's a celebration of the person we lost, the love he created, the differences he made with the limitations he had.

Robert's memorial service and the events leading up to it, sad though they were, also reminded us that he has been released from this world with all its suffering and pain. His problems are behind him. He is finally free.

In the end, Robert's untimely passing became a party. And that's exactly what he would have wanted.

OCTOBER 6, 2010

EPILOGUE

THE GROWING SEASON

The Peach Tree

I am routinely astounded this spring by the peach tree that flourishes in a corner of my backyard. It's a low, bushy affair, loaded to abundance with early fruit that weighs down the thin boughs. There must be hundreds of peaches forming in this tree, each beginning to sport a deep flush of red beneath downy white fuzz. When I circle the yard to sneak peeks at the tree or to pause in its shade with my lawnmower, I am every time struck by the powerful display of fertility and by a vivid mental image of the ripe, juicy peaches — my favorite fruit — that are to come.

I will pick them and wash them. I will boil them down into jelly or jam, press them for juice (and, perhaps, a little wine). I will puree them into a cold summertime soup, chop them, and bake them into pies. A few of them I will bite into fresh off the tree, allowing the juice to course down my chin and onto my shirt. And at some point there will be a tremendous cobbler, enough for all who want.

In the past I always bought my peaches at the store. I did not even realize that the tree in my yard was a peach tree until we had lived there five years. One June it seemingly burst into scads of golden and rosy fruit, mottled though it was with bug scars and skin rot. I decided then and there to see if I could coax edible fruit from the tree and its neighbor, a tall apricot tree planted on the slope.

Last year, I diligently pruned the boughs of each and purchased an organic bug spray that supremely reeked of rancid fish-head oil and Vitamin B. Both trees bloomed early last spring, but a late-season frost destroyed any hope of fruit. There was nothing to show for the year's growth save for curdled flower petals scattered on the icy ground.

But optimum conditions conspired this year for a banner crop — at least from the peach tree. The apricot tree has yet to follow suit.

I spent much time this past weekend looking at my peach tree. My wife and our daughter had gone down to Myrtle Beach for a girls' weekend with relatives while the boys and I were left home to make a go of it. The original plan was to bring the Xbox 360 to Winston-Salem and hole up in a hotel room stocked with cold drinks, salty snacks, and some form of chocolate. We would hunker down and give ourselves thumb cramps.

This was not to be: Graduation weekend, while a boon to local hoteliers, prevented us from securing a room. No matter — the boys and I loaded up the larder with thick-sliced country bacon, steaks, and farm eggs with double yolks. We picked up a few new video games, kicked a clear space on their bedroom floor, and set about mastering video challenges. In between there was a trip to a pizza buffet and an expedition to the history museum at Battleground Park accompanied by a walk through the wooded trails. But most of the time it was the two of them in their room locked in virtual combat while I did things like sort laundry, wash dishes, and walk the yard, pondering the significance of my fabulous peach tree.

The boys are coming along wonderfully, interfacing with the world around them with increasing sophistication, becoming kinder and more tolerant with each passing season, growing like they're getting paid to do it. I caught myself watching them this weekend, eavesdropping on their conversations, appreciating them in a way that I cannot when I'm trying to get them dressed and fed and on the bus in the morning or asking them to, for god's sake, please clean up that pigsty of a room.

It's amazing to me that these are my children, that somehow my wife and I have managed to bring them along this far without misplacing or seriously injuring them. We've been parents for just about ten years now, and it seems we're finally getting the hang of it.

Like the peaches that ripen in the corner of our yard after so many barren seasons, our children are starting to show the results of the better parts of their upbringing. There were missteps along the way, to be sure: a few cold winters to endure, some deficiencies to overcome, a host of external influences that required timely counter-measures. As farmers and as parents, we learn more every growing season.

Out in the yard, the peaches endure. They soak in the sun and rain, swell on the branches, and await their moment. Three weeks, I say. Four at the most. Then it's peach cobbler for everybody.

MAY 19, 2010

ABOUT THE AUTHOR

Brian Clarey is the founding editor of *YES! Weekly* in Greensboro, N.C., and has won awards for his editorials and his column, Crashing the Gate, from the N.C. Press Association. He previously covered the bar scene for *Triad Style* and *Go Triad,* and was a feature writer for *Where Y'at Magazine* in New Orleans.

He graduated from Loyola University with a B.A. in communications, and spent 10 years tending bar in New Orleans. A native of Garden City, Long Island, he is married and has three children.

For more information, visit www.brianclarey.com

ACKNOWLEDGMENTS

You wouldn't believe how many people it takes to put out a book, most of whom with tasks much more difficult than mine. None of this would have happened without Charles Womack, publisher of *YES! Weekly,* whose faith in me has enabled my whole career.

And the people at Cold Type Press deserve mention, chiefly Lorraine Ahearn, my friend who convinced me this was possible. Elma Sabo, book editor, gave my words way more attention than they're used to. Designer Elaine Shields brought savvy and discipline. And artist Margaret Baxter gave us the perfect look. Newspaper people, one and all, they never fold under deadline. Devender Sellars, *YES! Weekly's* art director, shot the cover with a little help from All Aces Media. And thanks goes to Doc and Danny at the Blind Tiger who let us use the room before the afternoon drinkers rolled in.

I could never have done any of this without a mother who loved books and a father who kept the house stocked with newspapers and magazines, so they get a piece of the credit. Behind me every step of the way have been my wife and children. I also must thank all of the people who trusted me with their stories over the years, and all of the people who read them. And it wouldn't feel right if I didn't give a shout-out to the folks down at Igor's in New Orleans, where classes start at 2 a.m. and last until well past sunrise.

IF YOU LIKED THIS BOOK...

Cold Type Press brings the perfect collection for the reader in your family:

The Man Who Became Santa Claus
and Other Winter Tales

What critics say about author Lorraine Ahearn, winner of the national Casey Award and the Associated Press Mark Twain Award for Investigative Reporting:

"Hers is the work of a journalist interested in reportorial discovery, and her reporting is superb. She's on the street, investing shoe leather, sticking notes in screen doors, talking to real people and listening to what they say. She obviously knows these stories before she ever touches a keyboard." — **Kevin Merida, The Washington Post**

"Reading these columns, I was moved more times per inch of type than I've been in a long time."
— **Diane Bacha, Milwaukee Journal Sentinel**

"Her insightful writing commands attention and fosters a connection between readers and the larger community... She uses a reporter's eyes and ears, a writer's voice and a columnist's heart to great effect."
— **Chip Scanlan, Poynter Institute**

Visit our website at lorraineahearn.com